C-854   CAREER EXAMINATION SERIES

This is your
PASSBOOK for...

Urban/ City Planner

Test Preparation Study Guide
Questions & Answers

COPYRIGHT NOTICE

This book is SOLELY intended for, is sold ONLY to, and its use is RESTRICTED to individual, bona fide applicants or candidates who qualify by virtue of having seriously filed applications for appropriate license, certificate, professional and/or promotional advancement, higher school matriculation, scholarship, or other legitimate requirements of education and/or governmental authorities.

This book is NOT intended for use, class instruction, tutoring, training, duplication, copying, reprinting, excerption, or adaptation, etc., by:

1) Other publishers
2) Proprietors and/or Instructors of "Coaching" and/or Preparatory Courses
3) Personnel and/or Training Divisions of commercial, industrial, and governmental organizations
4) Schools, colleges, or universities and/or their departments and staffs, including teachers and other personnel
5) Testing Agencies or Bureaus
6) Study groups which seek by the purchase of a single volume to copy and/or duplicate and/or adapt this material for use by the group as a whole without having purchased individual volumes for each of the members of the group
7) Et al.

Such persons would be in violation of appropriate Federal and State statutes.

PROVISION OF LICENSING AGREEMENTS – Recognized educational, commercial, industrial, and governmental institutions and organizations, and others legitimately engaged in educational pursuits, including training, testing, and measurement activities, may address request for a licensing agreement to the copyright owners, who will determine whether, and under what conditions, including fees and charges, the materials in this book may be used them. In other words, a licensing facility exists for the legitimate use of the material in this book on other than an individual basis. However, it is asseverated and affirmed here that the material in this book CANNOT be used without the receipt of the express permission of such a licensing agreement from the Publishers. Inquiries re licensing should be addressed to the company, attention rights and permissions department.

All rights reserved, including the right of reproduction in whole or in part, in any form or by any means, electronic or mechanical, including photocopying, recording, or by any information storage and retrieval system, without permission in writing from the Publisher.

Copyright © 2025 by
National Learning Corporation

212 Michael Drive, Syosset, NY 11791
(516) 921-8888 • www.passbooks.com
E-mail: info@passbooks.com

PASSBOOK® SERIES

THE *PASSBOOK® SERIES* has been created to prepare applicants and candidates for the ultimate academic battlefield – the examination room.

At some time in our lives, each and every one of us may be required to take an examination – for validation, matriculation, admission, qualification, registration, certification, or licensure.

Based on the assumption that every applicant or candidate has met the basic formal educational standards, has taken the required number of courses, and read the necessary texts, the *PASSBOOK® SERIES* furnishes the one special preparation which may assure passing with confidence, instead of failing with insecurity. Examination questions – together with answers – are furnished as the basic vehicle for study so that the mysteries of the examination and its compounding difficulties may be eliminated or diminished by a sure method.

This book is meant to help you pass your examination provided that you qualify and are serious in your objective.

The entire field is reviewed through the huge store of content information which is succinctly presented through a provocative and challenging approach – the question-and-answer method.

A climate of success is established by furnishing the correct answers at the end of each test.

You soon learn to recognize types of questions, forms of questions, and patterns of questioning. You may even begin to anticipate expected outcomes.

You perceive that many questions are repeated or adapted so that you can gain acute insights, which may enable you to score many sure points.

You learn how to confront new questions, or types of questions, and to attack them confidently and work out the correct answers.

You note objectives and emphases, and recognize pitfalls and dangers, so that you may make positive educational adjustments.

Moreover, you are kept fully informed in relation to new concepts, methods, practices, and directions in the field.

You discover that you are actually taking the examination all the time: you are preparing for the examination by "taking" an examination, not by reading extraneous and/or supererogatory textbooks.

In short, this PASSBOOK®, used directedly, should be an important factor in helping you to pass your test.

URBAN (CITY) PLANNER

JOB DESCRIPTION

Under supervision, with latitude for independent judgment, organizes and/or performs research and analysis activities of varying degrees of difficulty in the field of city planning. Performs related work.

EXAMPLES OF TYPICAL TASKS

Organizes and conducts planning studies in order to identify issues and solve problems. Reviews land use, housing, transportation, environmental and other planning proposals and applications to ensure compliance with government regulations and policies. Defines information needs and sources and maintains organized data base of city functions, local area conditions and needs, for policy studies, community plans, land use and budget proposal reviews. Develops and carries out planning projects, including data collection, developing work programs, maintaining work schedules, coordinating intra and interagency activities, and recommending appropriate actions. Meets with applicants, consultants, community groups, agency staff and others to present the objectives, techniques and implications of city planning and to evaluate and resolve planning and technical issues. Uses computers to analyze data and prepare reports. Make recommendations based on summary and analysis of data. Prepares diagrams, drawings and graphics related to planning studies. Prepares related reports, studies and other written documents.

SCOPE OF THE EXAMINATION

The multiple-choice test will cover knowledge, skills and abilities in such areas as sociological, economic, design and environmental factors involved in physical planning and community development; principles and practices of urban planning; collection, analysis and presentation of data as related to planning; understanding and interpreting maps, charts and graphs; understanding and interpreting written material; and will assess the ability to apply land use, housing, transportation, environmental and other applicable regulations, principles, policies and procedures; the ability to apply planning theory and principles; knowledge of research techniques and methodology; the ability to prepare for presentations; written communication skills; knowledge of, and ability to use quantitative techniques; the ability to analyze material to draw conclusions and makerecommendations; the ability to develop a work program or project; and other related areas.

HOW TO TAKE A TEST

I. YOU MUST PASS AN EXAMINATION

A. *WHAT EVERY CANDIDATE SHOULD KNOW*

Examination applicants often ask us for help in preparing for the written test. What can I study in advance? What kinds of questions will be asked? How will the test be given? How will the papers be graded?

As an applicant for a civil service examination, you may be wondering about some of these things. Our purpose here is to suggest effective methods of advance study and to describe civil service examinations.

Your chances for success on this examination can be increased if you know how to prepare. Those "pre-examination jitters" can be reduced if you know what to expect. You can even experience an adventure in good citizenship if you know why civil service exams are given.

B. *WHY ARE CIVIL SERVICE EXAMINATIONS GIVEN?*

Civil service examinations are important to you in two ways. As a citizen, you want public jobs filled by employees who know how to do their work. As a job seeker, you want a fair chance to compete for that job on an equal footing with other candidates. The best-known means of accomplishing this two-fold goal is the competitive examination.

Exams are widely publicized throughout the nation. They may be administered for jobs in federal, state, city, municipal, town or village governments or agencies.

Any citizen may apply, with some limitations, such as the age or residence of applicants. Your experience and education may be reviewed to see whether you meet the requirements for the particular examination. When these requirements exist, they are reasonable and applied consistently to all applicants. Thus, a competitive examination may cause you some uneasiness now, but it is your privilege and safeguard.

C. *HOW ARE CIVIL SERVICE EXAMS DEVELOPED?*

Examinations are carefully written by trained technicians who are specialists in the field known as "psychological measurement," in consultation with recognized authorities in the field of work that the test will cover. These experts recommend the subject matter areas or skills to be tested; only those knowledges or skills important to your success on the job are included. The most reliable books and source materials available are used as references. Together, the experts and technicians judge the difficulty level of the questions.

Test technicians know how to phrase questions so that the problem is clearly stated. Their ethics do not permit "trick" or "catch" questions. Questions may have been tried out on sample groups, or subjected to statistical analysis, to determine their usefulness.

Written tests are often used in combination with performance tests, ratings of training and experience, and oral interviews. All of these measures combine to form the best-known means of finding the right person for the right job.

II. HOW TO PASS THE WRITTEN TEST

A. NATURE OF THE EXAMINATION

To prepare intelligently for civil service examinations, you should know how they differ from school examinations you have taken. In school you were assigned certain definite pages to read or subjects to cover. The examination questions were quite detailed and usually emphasized memory. Civil service exams, on the other hand, try to discover your present ability to perform the duties of a position, plus your potentiality to learn these duties. In other words, a civil service exam attempts to predict how successful you will be. Questions cover such a broad area that they cannot be as minute and detailed as school exam questions.

In the public service similar kinds of work, or positions, are grouped together in one "class." This process is known as *position-classification*. All the positions in a class are paid according to the salary range for that class. One class title covers all of these positions, and they are all tested by the same examination.

B. FOUR BASIC STEPS

1) Study the announcement

How, then, can you know what subjects to study? Our best answer is: "Learn as much as possible about the class of positions for which you've applied." The exam will test the knowledge, skills and abilities needed to do the work.

Your most valuable source of information about the position you want is the official exam announcement. This announcement lists the training and experience qualifications. Check these standards and apply only if you come reasonably close to meeting them.

The brief description of the position in the examination announcement offers some clues to the subjects which will be tested. Think about the job itself. Review the duties in your mind. Can you perform them, or are there some in which you are rusty? Fill in the blank spots in your preparation.

Many jurisdictions preview the written test in the exam announcement by including a section called "Knowledge and Abilities Required," "Scope of the Examination," or some similar heading. Here you will find out specifically what fields will be tested.

2) Review your own background

Once you learn in general what the position is all about, and what you need to know to do the work, ask yourself which subjects you already know fairly well and which need improvement. You may wonder whether to concentrate on improving your strong areas or on building some background in your fields of weakness. When the announcement has specified "some knowledge" or "considerable knowledge," or has used adjectives like "beginning principles of..." or "advanced ... methods," you can get a clue as to the number and difficulty of questions to be asked in any given field. More questions, and hence broader coverage, would be included for those subjects which are more important in the work. Now weigh your strengths and weaknesses against the job requirements and prepare accordingly.

3) Determine the level of the position

Another way to tell how intensively you should prepare is to understand the level of the job for which you are applying. Is it the entering level? In other words, is this the position in which beginners in a field of work are hired? Or is it an intermediate or advanced level? Sometimes this is indicated by such words as "Junior" or "Senior" in the class title. Other jurisdictions use Roman numerals to designate the level – Clerk I, Clerk II, for example. The word "Supervisor" sometimes appears in the title. If the level is not indicated by the title, check the description of duties. Will you be working under very close supervision, or will you have responsibility for independent decisions in this work?

4) Choose appropriate study materials

Now that you know the subjects to be examined and the relative amount of each subject to be covered, you can choose suitable study materials. For beginning level jobs, or even advanced ones, if you have a pronounced weakness in some aspect of your training, read a modern, standard textbook in that field. Be sure it is up to date and has general coverage. Such books are normally available at your library, and the librarian will be glad to help you locate one. For entry-level positions, questions of appropriate difficulty are chosen – neither highly advanced questions, nor those too simple. Such questions require careful thought but not advanced training.

If the position for which you are applying is technical or advanced, you will read more advanced, specialized material. If you are already familiar with the basic principles of your field, elementary textbooks would waste your time. Concentrate on advanced textbooks and technical periodicals. Think through the concepts and review difficult problems in your field.

These are all general sources. You can get more ideas on your own initiative, following these leads. For example, training manuals and publications of the government agency which employs workers in your field can be useful, particularly for technical and professional positions. A letter or visit to the government department involved may result in more specific study suggestions, and certainly will provide you with a more definite idea of the exact nature of the position you are seeking.

III. KINDS OF TESTS

Tests are used for purposes other than measuring knowledge and ability to perform specified duties. For some positions, it is equally important to test ability to make adjustments to new situations or to profit from training. In others, basic mental abilities not dependent on information are essential. Questions which test these things may not appear as pertinent to the duties of the position as those which test for knowledge and information. Yet they are often highly important parts of a fair examination. For very general questions, it is almost impossible to help you direct your study efforts. What we can do is to point out some of the more common of these general abilities needed in public service positions and describe some typical questions.

1) General Information

Broad, general information has been found useful for predicting job success in some kinds of work. This is tested in a variety of ways, from vocabulary lists to questions about current events. Basic background in some field of work, such as sociology or economics, may be sampled in a group of questions. Often these are principles which have become familiar to most persons through exposure rather than through formal training. It is difficult to advise you how to study for these questions; being alert to the world around you is our best suggestion.

2) Verbal ability

An example of an ability needed in many positions is verbal or language ability. Verbal ability is, in brief, the ability to use and understand words. Vocabulary and grammar tests are typical measures of this ability. Reading comprehension or paragraph interpretation questions are common in many kinds of civil service tests. You are given a paragraph of written material and asked to find its central meaning.

3) Numerical ability

Number skills can be tested by the familiar arithmetic problem, by checking paired lists of numbers to see which are alike and which are different, or by interpreting charts and graphs. In the latter test, a graph may be printed in the test booklet which you are asked to use as the basis for answering questions.

4) Observation

A popular test for law-enforcement positions is the observation test. A picture is shown to you for several minutes, then taken away. Questions about the picture test your ability to observe both details and larger elements.

5) Following directions

In many positions in the public service, the employee must be able to carry out written instructions dependably and accurately. You may be given a chart with several columns, each column listing a variety of information. The questions require you to carry out directions involving the information given in the chart.

6) Skills and aptitudes

Performance tests effectively measure some manual skills and aptitudes. When the skill is one in which you are trained, such as typing or shorthand, you can practice. These tests are often very much like those given in business school or high school courses. For many of the other skills and aptitudes, however, no short-time preparation can be made. Skills and abilities natural to you or that you have developed throughout your lifetime are being tested.

Many of the general questions just described provide all the data needed to answer the questions and ask you to use your reasoning ability to find the answers. Your best preparation for these tests, as well as for tests of facts and ideas, is to be at your physical and mental best. You, no doubt, have your own methods of getting into an exam-taking mood and keeping "in shape." The next section lists some ideas on this subject.

IV. KINDS OF QUESTIONS

Only rarely is the "essay" question, which you answer in narrative form, used in civil service tests. Civil service tests are usually of the short-answer type. Full instructions for answering these questions will be given to you at the examination. But in case this is your first experience with short-answer questions and separate answer sheets, here is what you need to know:

1) Multiple-choice Questions

Most popular of the short-answer questions is the "multiple choice" or "best answer" question. It can be used, for example, to test for factual knowledge, ability to solve problems or judgment in meeting situations found at work.

A multiple-choice question is normally one of three types—
- It can begin with an incomplete statement followed by several possible endings. You are to find the one ending which *best* completes the statement, although some of the others may not be entirely wrong.
- It can also be a complete statement in the form of a question which is answered by choosing one of the statements listed.

- It can be in the form of a problem – again you select the best answer.

Here is an example of a multiple-choice question with a discussion which should give you some clues as to the method for choosing the right answer:

When an employee has a complaint about his assignment, the action which will *best* help him overcome his difficulty is to
  A. discuss his difficulty with his coworkers
  B. take the problem to the head of the organization
  C. take the problem to the person who gave him the assignment
  D. say nothing to anyone about his complaint

In answering this question, you should study each of the choices to find which is best. Consider choice "A" – Certainly an employee may discuss his complaint with fellow employees, but no change or improvement can result, and the complaint remains unresolved. Choice "B" is a poor choice since the head of the organization probably does not know what assignment you have been given, and taking your problem to him is known as "going over the head" of the supervisor. The supervisor, or person who made the assignment, is the person who can clarify it or correct any injustice. Choice "C" is, therefore, correct. To say nothing, as in choice "D," is unwise. Supervisors have and interest in knowing the problems employees are facing, and the employee is seeking a solution to his problem.

2) True/False Questions

The "true/false" or "right/wrong" form of question is sometimes used. Here a complete statement is given. Your job is to decide whether the statement is right or wrong.

SAMPLE: A roaming cell-phone call to a nearby city costs less than a non-roaming call to a distant city.

This statement is wrong, or false, since roaming calls are more expensive.

This is not a complete list of all possible question forms, although most of the others are variations of these common types. You will always get complete directions for answering questions. Be sure you understand *how* to mark your answers – ask questions until you do.

V. RECORDING YOUR ANSWERS

Computer terminals are used more and more today for many different kinds of exams.
For an examination with very few applicants, you may be told to record your answers in the test booklet itself. Separate answer sheets are much more common. If this separate answer sheet is to be scored by machine – and this is often the case – it is highly important that you mark your answers correctly in order to get credit.
An electronic scoring machine is often used in civil service offices because of the speed with which papers can be scored. Machine-scored answer sheets must be marked with a pencil, which will be given to you. This pencil has a high graphite content which responds to the electronic scoring machine. As a matter of fact, stray dots may register as answers, so do not let your pencil rest on the answer sheet while you are pondering the correct answer. Also, if your pencil lead breaks or is otherwise defective, ask for another.

Since the answer sheet will be dropped in a slot in the scoring machine, be careful not to bend the corners or get the paper crumpled.

The answer sheet normally has five vertical columns of numbers, with 30 numbers to a column. These numbers correspond to the question numbers in your test booklet. After each number, going across the page are four or five pairs of dotted lines. These short dotted lines have small letters or numbers above them. The first two pairs may also have a "T" or "F" above the letters. This indicates that the first two pairs only are to be used if the questions are of the true-false type. If the questions are multiple choice, disregard the "T" and "F" and pay attention only to the small letters or numbers.

Answer your questions in the manner of the sample that follows:

32. The largest city in the United States is
    A. Washington, D.C.
    B. New York City
    C. Chicago
    D. Detroit
    E. San Francisco

1) Choose the answer you think is best. (New York City is the largest, so "B" is correct.)
2) Find the row of dotted lines numbered the same as the question you are answering. (Find row number 32)
3) Find the pair of dotted lines corresponding to the answer. (Find the pair of lines under the mark "B.")
4) Make a solid black mark between the dotted lines.

VI. BEFORE THE TEST

Common sense will help you find procedures to follow to get ready for an examination. Too many of us, however, overlook these sensible measures. Indeed, nervousness and fatigue have been found to be the most serious reasons why applicants fail to do their best on civil service tests. Here is a list of reminders:

- Begin your preparation early – Don't wait until the last minute to go scurrying around for books and materials or to find out what the position is all about.
- Prepare continuously – An hour a night for a week is better than an all-night cram session. This has been definitely established. What is more, a night a week for a month will return better dividends than crowding your study into a shorter period of time.
- Locate the place of the exam – You have been sent a notice telling you when and where to report for the examination. If the location is in a different town or otherwise unfamiliar to you, it would be well to inquire the best route and learn something about the building.
- Relax the night before the test – Allow your mind to rest. Do not study at all that night. Plan some mild recreation or diversion; then go to bed early and get a good night's sleep.
- Get up early enough to make a leisurely trip to the place for the test – This way unforeseen events, traffic snarls, unfamiliar buildings, etc. will not upset you.
- Dress comfortably – A written test is not a fashion show. You will be known by number and not by name, so wear something comfortable.

- Leave excess paraphernalia at home – Shopping bags and odd bundles will get in your way. You need bring only the items mentioned in the official notice you received; usually everything you need is provided. Do not bring reference books to the exam. They will only confuse those last minutes and be taken away from you when in the test room.
- Arrive somewhat ahead of time – If because of transportation schedules you must get there very early, bring a newspaper or magazine to take your mind off yourself while waiting.
- Locate the examination room – When you have found the proper room, you will be directed to the seat or part of the room where you will sit. Sometimes you are given a sheet of instructions to read while you are waiting. Do not fill out any forms until you are told to do so; just read them and be prepared.
- Relax and prepare to listen to the instructions
- If you have any physical problem that may keep you from doing your best, be sure to tell the test administrator. If you are sick or in poor health, you really cannot do your best on the exam. You can come back and take the test some other time.

VII. AT THE TEST

The day of the test is here and you have the test booklet in your hand. The temptation to get going is very strong. Caution! There is more to success than knowing the right answers. You must know how to identify your papers and understand variations in the type of short-answer question used in this particular examination. Follow these suggestions for maximum results from your efforts:

1) Cooperate with the monitor

The test administrator has a duty to create a situation in which you can be as much at ease as possible. He will give instructions, tell you when to begin, check to see that you are marking your answer sheet correctly, and so on. He is not there to guard you, although he will see that your competitors do not take unfair advantage. He wants to help you do your best.

2) Listen to all instructions

Don't jump the gun! Wait until you understand all directions. In most civil service tests you get more time than you need to answer the questions. So don't be in a hurry. Read each word of instructions until you clearly understand the meaning. Study the examples, listen to all announcements and follow directions. Ask questions if you do not understand what to do.

3) Identify your papers

Civil service exams are usually identified by number only. You will be assigned a number; you must not put your name on your test papers. Be sure to copy your number correctly. Since more than one exam may be given, copy your exact examination title.

4) Plan your time

Unless you are told that a test is a "speed" or "rate of work" test, speed itself is usually not important. Time enough to answer all the questions will be provided, but this does not mean that you have all day. An overall time limit has been set. Divide the total time (in minutes) by the number of questions to determine the approximate time you have for each question.

5) Do not linger over difficult questions

If you come across a difficult question, mark it with a paper clip (useful to have along) and come back to it when you have been through the booklet. One caution if you do this – be sure to skip a number on your answer sheet as well. Check often to be sure that you have not lost your place and that you are marking in the row numbered the same as the question you are answering.

6) Read the questions

Be sure you know what the question asks! Many capable people are unsuccessful because they failed to *read* the questions correctly.

7) Answer all questions

Unless you have been instructed that a penalty will be deducted for incorrect answers, it is better to guess than to omit a question.

8) Speed tests

It is often better NOT to guess on speed tests. It has been found that on timed tests people are tempted to spend the last few seconds before time is called in marking answers at random – without even reading them – in the hope of picking up a few extra points. To discourage this practice, the instructions may warn you that your score will be "corrected" for guessing. That is, a penalty will be applied. The incorrect answers will be deducted from the correct ones, or some other penalty formula will be used.

9) Review your answers

If you finish before time is called, go back to the questions you guessed or omitted to give them further thought. Review other answers if you have time.

10) Return your test materials

If you are ready to leave before others have finished or time is called, take ALL your materials to the monitor and leave quietly. Never take any test material with you. The monitor can discover whose papers are not complete, and taking a test booklet may be grounds for disqualification.

VIII. EXAMINATION TECHNIQUES

1) Read the general instructions carefully. These are usually printed on the first page of the exam booklet. As a rule, these instructions refer to the timing of the examination; the fact that you should not start work until the signal and must stop work at a signal, etc. If there are any *special* instructions, such as a choice of questions to be answered, make sure that you note this instruction carefully.

2) When you are ready to start work on the examination, that is as soon as the signal has been given, read the instructions to each question booklet, underline any key words or phrases, such as *least, best, outline, describe* and the like. In this way you will tend to answer as requested rather than discover on reviewing your paper that you *listed without describing*, that you selected the *worst* choice rather than the *best* choice, etc.

3) If the examination is of the objective or multiple-choice type – that is, each question will also give a series of possible answers: A, B, C or D, and you are called upon to select the best answer and write the letter next to that answer on your answer paper – it is advisable to start answering each question in turn. There may be anywhere from 50 to 100 such questions in the three or four hours allotted and you can see how much time would be taken if you read through all the questions before beginning to answer any. Furthermore, if you come across a question or group of questions which you know would be difficult to answer, it would undoubtedly affect your handling of all the other questions.

4) If the examination is of the essay type and contains but a few questions, it is a moot point as to whether you should read all the questions before starting to answer any one. Of course, if you are given a choice – say five out of seven and the like – then it is essential to read all the questions so you can eliminate the two that are most difficult. If, however, you are asked to answer all the questions, there may be danger in trying to answer the easiest one first because you may find that you will spend too much time on it. The best technique is to answer the first question, then proceed to the second, etc.

5) Time your answers. Before the exam begins, write down the time it started, then add the time allowed for the examination and write down the time it must be completed, then divide the time available somewhat as follows:
    - If 3-1/2 hours are allowed, that would be 210 minutes. If you have 80 objective-type questions, that would be an average of 2-1/2 minutes per question. Allow yourself no more than 2 minutes per question, or a total of 160 minutes, which will permit about 50 minutes to review.
    - If for the time allotment of 210 minutes there are 7 essay questions to answer, that would average about 30 minutes a question. Give yourself only 25 minutes per question so that you have about 35 minutes to review.

6) The most important instruction is to *read each question* and make sure you know what is wanted. The second most important instruction is to *time yourself properly* so that you answer every question. The third most important instruction is to *answer every question*. Guess if you have to but include something for each question. Remember that you will receive no credit for a blank and will probably receive some credit if you write something in answer to an essay question. If you guess a letter – say "B" for a multiple-choice question – you may have guessed right. If you leave a blank as an answer to a multiple-choice question, the examiners may respect your feelings but it will not add a point to your score. Some exams may penalize you for wrong answers, so in such cases *only*, you may not want to guess unless you have some basis for your answer.

7) Suggestions
    a. Objective-type questions
        1. Examine the question booklet for proper sequence of pages and questions
        2. Read all instructions carefully
        3. Skip any question which seems too difficult; return to it after all other questions have been answered
        4. Apportion your time properly; do not spend too much time on any single question or group of questions

5. Note and underline key words – *all, most, fewest, least, best, worst, same, opposite,* etc.
6. Pay particular attention to negatives
7. Note unusual option, e.g., unduly long, short, complex, different or similar in content to the body of the question
8. Observe the use of "hedging" words – *probably, may, most likely,* etc.
9. Make sure that your answer is put next to the same number as the question
10. Do not second-guess unless you have good reason to believe the second answer is definitely more correct
11. Cross out original answer if you decide another answer is more accurate; do not erase until you are ready to hand your paper in
12. Answer all questions; guess unless instructed otherwise
13. Leave time for review

b. Essay questions
1. Read each question carefully
2. Determine exactly what is wanted. Underline key words or phrases.
3. Decide on outline or paragraph answer
4. Include many different points and elements unless asked to develop any one or two points or elements
5. Show impartiality by giving pros and cons unless directed to select one side only
6. Make and write down any assumptions you find necessary to answer the questions
7. Watch your English, grammar, punctuation and choice of words
8. Time your answers; don't crowd material

8) Answering the essay question

Most essay questions can be answered by framing the specific response around several key words or ideas. Here are a few such key words or ideas:

M's: manpower, materials, methods, money, management
P's: purpose, program, policy, plan, procedure, practice, problems, pitfalls, personnel, public relations

a. Six basic steps in handling problems:
1. Preliminary plan and background development
2. Collect information, data and facts
3. Analyze and interpret information, data and facts
4. Analyze and develop solutions as well as make recommendations
5. Prepare report and sell recommendations
6. Install recommendations and follow up effectiveness

b. Pitfalls to avoid
1. *Taking things for granted* – A statement of the situation does not necessarily imply that each of the elements is necessarily true; for example, a complaint may be invalid and biased so that all that can be taken for granted is that a complaint has been registered

2. *Considering only one side of a situation* – Wherever possible, indicate several alternatives and then point out the reasons you selected the best one
3. *Failing to indicate follow up* – Whenever your answer indicates action on your part, make certain that you will take proper follow-up action to see how successful your recommendations, procedures or actions turn out to be
4. *Taking too long in answering any single question* – Remember to time your answers properly

IX. AFTER THE TEST

Scoring procedures differ in detail among civil service jurisdictions although the general principles are the same. Whether the papers are hand-scored or graded by machine we have described, they are nearly always graded by number. That is, the person who marks the paper knows only the number – never the name – of the applicant. Not until all the papers have been graded will they be matched with names. If other tests, such as training and experience or oral interview ratings have been given, scores will be combined. Different parts of the examination usually have different weights. For example, the written test might count 60 percent of the final grade, and a rating of training and experience 40 percent. In many jurisdictions, veterans will have a certain number of points added to their grades.

After the final grade has been determined, the names are placed in grade order and an eligible list is established. There are various methods for resolving ties between those who get the same final grade – probably the most common is to place first the name of the person whose application was received first. Job offers are made from the eligible list in the order the names appear on it. You will be notified of your grade and your rank as soon as all these computations have been made. This will be done as rapidly as possible.

People who are found to meet the requirements in the announcement are called "eligibles." Their names are put on a list of eligible candidates. An eligible's chances of getting a job depend on how high he stands on this list and how fast agencies are filling jobs from the list.

When a job is to be filled from a list of eligibles, the agency asks for the names of people on the list of eligibles for that job. When the civil service commission receives this request, it sends to the agency the names of the three people highest on this list. Or, if the job to be filled has specialized requirements, the office sends the agency the names of the top three persons who meet these requirements from the general list.

The appointing officer makes a choice from among the three people whose names were sent to him. If the selected person accepts the appointment, the names of the others are put back on the list to be considered for future openings.

That is the rule in hiring from all kinds of eligible lists, whether they are for typist, carpenter, chemist, or something else. For every vacancy, the appointing officer has his choice of any one of the top three eligibles on the list. This explains why the person whose name is on top of the list sometimes does not get an appointment when some of the persons lower on the list do. If the appointing officer chooses the second or third eligible, the No. 1 eligible does not get a job at once, but stays on the list until he is appointed or the list is terminated.

X. HOW TO PASS THE INTERVIEW TEST

The examination for which you applied requires an oral interview test. You have already taken the written test and you are now being called for the interview test – the final part of the formal examination.

You may think that it is not possible to prepare for an interview test and that there are no procedures to follow during an interview. Our purpose is to point out some things you can do in advance that will help you and some good rules to follow and pitfalls to avoid while you are being interviewed.

What is an interview supposed to test?

The written examination is designed to test the technical knowledge and competence of the candidate; the oral is designed to evaluate intangible qualities, not readily measured otherwise, and to establish a list showing the relative fitness of each candidate – as measured against his competitors – for the position sought. Scoring is not on the basis of "right" and "wrong," but on a sliding scale of values ranging from "not passable" to "outstanding." As a matter of fact, it is possible to achieve a relatively low score without a single "incorrect" answer because of evident weakness in the qualities being measured.

Occasionally, an examination may consist entirely of an oral test – either an individual or a group oral. In such cases, information is sought concerning the technical knowledges and abilities of the candidate, since there has been no written examination for this purpose. More commonly, however, an oral test is used to supplement a written examination.

Who conducts interviews?

The composition of oral boards varies among different jurisdictions. In nearly all, a representative of the personnel department serves as chairman. One of the members of the board may be a representative of the department in which the candidate would work. In some cases, "outside experts" are used, and, frequently, a businessman or some other representative of the general public is asked to serve. Labor and management or other special groups may be represented. The aim is to secure the services of experts in the appropriate field.

However the board is composed, it is a good idea (and not at all improper or unethical) to ascertain in advance of the interview who the members are and what groups they represent. When you are introduced to them, you will have some idea of their backgrounds and interests, and at least you will not stutter and stammer over their names.

What should be done before the interview?

While knowledge about the board members is useful and takes some of the surprise element out of the interview, there is other preparation which is more substantive. It *is* possible to prepare for an oral interview – in several ways:

1) Keep a copy of your application and review it carefully before the interview

This may be the only document before the oral board, and the starting point of the interview. Know what education and experience you have listed there, and the sequence and dates of all of it. Sometimes the board will ask you to review the highlights of your experience for them; you should not have to hem and haw doing it.

2) Study the class specification and the examination announcement

Usually, the oral board has one or both of these to guide them. The qualities, characteristics or knowledges required by the position sought are stated in these documents. They offer valuable clues as to the nature of the oral interview. For example, if the job involves supervisory responsibilities, the announcement will usually indicate that knowledge of modern supervisory methods and the qualifications of the candidate as a supervisor will be tested. If so, you can expect such questions, frequently in the form of a hypothetical situation which you are expected to solve. NEVER go into an oral without knowledge of the duties and responsibilities of the job you seek.

3) Think through each qualification required

Try to visualize the kind of questions you would ask if you were a board member. How well could you answer them? Try especially to appraise your own knowledge and background in each area, *measured against the job sought*, and identify any areas in which you are weak. Be critical and realistic – do not flatter yourself.

4) Do some general reading in areas in which you feel you may be weak

For example, if the job involves supervision and your past experience has NOT, some general reading in supervisory methods and practices, particularly in the field of human relations, might be useful. Do NOT study agency procedures or detailed manuals. The oral board will be testing your understanding and capacity, not your memory.

5) Get a good night's sleep and watch your general health and mental attitude

You will want a clear head at the interview. Take care of a cold or any other minor ailment, and of course, no hangovers.

What should be done on the day of the interview?

Now comes the day of the interview itself. Give yourself plenty of time to get there. Plan to arrive somewhat ahead of the scheduled time, particularly if your appointment is in the fore part of the day. If a previous candidate fails to appear, the board might be ready for you a bit early. By early afternoon an oral board is almost invariably behind schedule if there are many candidates, and you may have to wait. Take along a book or magazine to read, or your application to review, but leave any extraneous material in the waiting room when you go in for your interview. In any event, relax and compose yourself.

The matter of dress is important. The board is forming impressions about you – from your experience, your manners, your attitude, and your appearance. Give your personal appearance careful attention. Dress your best, but not your flashiest. Choose conservative, appropriate clothing, and be sure it is immaculate. This is a business interview, and your appearance should indicate that you regard it as such. Besides, being well groomed and properly dressed will help boost your confidence.

Sooner or later, someone will call your name and escort you into the interview room. *This is it.* From here on you are on your own. It is too late for any more preparation. But remember, you asked for this opportunity to prove your fitness, and you are here because your request was granted.

What happens when you go in?

The usual sequence of events will be as follows: The clerk (who is often the board stenographer) will introduce you to the chairman of the oral board, who will introduce you to the other members of the board. Acknowledge the introductions before you sit down. Do not be surprised if you find a microphone facing you or a stenotypist sitting by. Oral interviews are usually recorded in the event of an appeal or other review.

Usually the chairman of the board will open the interview by reviewing the highlights of your education and work experience from your application – primarily for the benefit of the other members of the board, as well as to get the material into the record. Do not interrupt or comment unless there is an error or significant misinterpretation; if that is the case, do not hesitate. But do not quibble about insignificant matters. Also, he will usually ask you some question about your education, experience or your present job – partly to get you to start talking and to establish the interviewing "rapport." He may start the actual questioning, or turn it over to one of the other members. Frequently, each member undertakes the questioning on a particular area, one in which he is perhaps most competent, so you can expect each member to participate in the examination. Because time is limited, you may also expect some rather abrupt switches in the direction the questioning takes, so do not be upset by it. Normally, a board member will not pursue a single line of questioning unless he discovers a particular strength or weakness.

After each member has participated, the chairman will usually ask whether any member has any further questions, then will ask you if you have anything you wish to add. Unless you are expecting this question, it may floor you. Worse, it may start you off on an extended, extemporaneous speech. The board is not usually seeking more information. The question is principally to offer you a last opportunity to present further qualifications or to indicate that you have nothing to add. So, if you feel that a significant qualification or characteristic has been overlooked, it is proper to point it out in a sentence or so. Do not compliment the board on the thoroughness of their examination – they have been sketchy, and you know it. If you wish, merely say, "No thank you, I have nothing further to add." This is a point where you can "talk yourself out" of a good impression or fail to present an important bit of information. Remember, *you close the interview yourself.*

The chairman will then say, "That is all, Mr. _____, thank you." Do not be startled; the interview is over, and quicker than you think. Thank him, gather your belongings and take your leave. Save your sigh of relief for the other side of the door.

How to put your best foot forward

Throughout this entire process, you may feel that the board individually and collectively is trying to pierce your defenses, seek out your hidden weaknesses and embarrass and confuse you. Actually, this is not true. They are obliged to make an appraisal of your qualifications for the job you are seeking, and they want to see you in your best light. Remember, they must interview all candidates and a non-cooperative candidate may become a failure in spite of their best efforts to bring out his qualifications. Here are 15 suggestions that will help you:

1) **Be natural – Keep your attitude confident, not cocky**

If you are not confident that you can do the job, do not expect the board to be. Do not apologize for your weaknesses, try to bring out your strong points. The board is interested in a positive, not negative, presentation. Cockiness will antagonize any board member and make him wonder if you are covering up a weakness by a false show of strength.

2) **Get comfortable, but don't lounge or sprawl**

Sit erectly but not stiffly. A careless posture may lead the board to conclude that you are careless in other things, or at least that you are not impressed by the importance of the occasion. Either conclusion is natural, even if incorrect. Do not fuss with your clothing, a pencil or an ashtray. Your hands may occasionally be useful to emphasize a point; do not let them become a point of distraction.

3) **Do not wisecrack or make small talk**

This is a serious situation, and your attitude should show that you consider it as such. Further, the time of the board is limited – they do not want to waste it, and neither should you.

4) Do not exaggerate your experience or abilities

In the first place, from information in the application or other interviews and sources, the board may know more about you than you think. Secondly, you probably will not get away with it. An experienced board is rather adept at spotting such a situation, so do not take the chance.

5) If you know a board member, do not make a point of it, yet do not hide it

Certainly you are not fooling him, and probably not the other members of the board. Do not try to take advantage of your acquaintanceship – it will probably do you little good.

6) Do not dominate the interview

Let the board do that. They will give you the clues – do not assume that you have to do all the talking. Realize that the board has a number of questions to ask you, and do not try to take up all the interview time by showing off your extensive knowledge of the answer to the first one.

7) Be attentive

You only have 20 minutes or so, and you should keep your attention at its sharpest throughout. When a member is addressing a problem or question to you, give him your undivided attention. Address your reply principally to him, but do not exclude the other board members.

8) Do not interrupt

A board member may be stating a problem for you to analyze. He will ask you a question when the time comes. Let him state the problem, and wait for the question.

9) Make sure you understand the question

Do not try to answer until you are sure what the question is. If it is not clear, restate it in your own words or ask the board member to clarify it for you. However, do not haggle about minor elements.

10) Reply promptly but not hastily

A common entry on oral board rating sheets is "candidate responded readily," or "candidate hesitated in replies." Respond as promptly and quickly as you can, but do not jump to a hasty, ill-considered answer.

11) Do not be peremptory in your answers

A brief answer is proper – but do not fire your answer back. That is a losing game from your point of view. The board member can probably ask questions much faster than you can answer them.

12) Do not try to create the answer you think the board member wants

He is interested in what kind of mind you have and how it works – not in playing games. Furthermore, he can usually spot this practice and will actually grade you down on it.

13) Do not switch sides in your reply merely to agree with a board member

Frequently, a member will take a contrary position merely to draw you out and to see if you are willing and able to defend your point of view. Do not start a debate, yet do not surrender a good position. If a position is worth taking, it is worth defending.

14) Do not be afraid to admit an error in judgment if you are shown to be wrong

The board knows that you are forced to reply without any opportunity for careful consideration. Your answer may be demonstrably wrong. If so, admit it and get on with the interview.

15) Do not dwell at length on your present job

The opening question may relate to your present assignment. Answer the question but do not go into an extended discussion. You are being examined for a *new* job, not your present one. As a matter of fact, try to phrase ALL your answers in terms of the job for which you are being examined.

Basis of Rating

Probably you will forget most of these "do's" and "don'ts" when you walk into the oral interview room. Even remembering them all will not ensure you a passing grade. Perhaps you did not have the qualifications in the first place. But remembering them will help you to put your best foot forward, without treading on the toes of the board members.

Rumor and popular opinion to the contrary notwithstanding, an oral board wants you to make the best appearance possible. They know you are under pressure – but they also want to see how you respond to it as a guide to what your reaction would be under the pressures of the job you seek. They will be influenced by the degree of poise you display, the personal traits you show and the manner in which you respond.

ABOUT THIS BOOK

This book contains tests divided into Examination Sections. Go through each test, answering every question in the margin. We have also attached a sample answer sheet at the back of the book that can be removed and used. At the end of each test look at the answer key and check your answers. On the ones you got wrong, look at the right answer choice and learn. Do not fill in the answers first. Do not memorize the questions and answers, but understand the answer and principles involved. On your test, the questions will likely be different from the samples. Questions are changed and new ones added. If you understand these past questions you should have success with any changes that arise. Tests may consist of several types of questions. We have additional books on each subject should more study be advisable or necessary for you. Finally, the more you study, the better prepared you will be. This book is intended to be the last thing you study before you walk into the examination room. Prior study of relevant texts is also recommended. NLC publishes some of these in our Fundamental Series. Knowledge and good sense are important factors in passing your exam. Good luck also helps. So now study this Passbook, absorb the material contained within and take that knowledge into the examination. Then do your best to pass that exam.

EXAMINATION SECTION

EXAMINATION SECTION
TEST 1

DIRECTIONS: Each question or incomplete statement is followed by several suggested answers or completions. Select the one that BEST answers the question or completes the Statement. *PRINT THE LETTER OF THE CORRECT ANSWER IN THE SPACE AT THE RIGHT.*

1. City planning should aim at

    A. over-all planning
    B. administrative planning
    C. planning of only physical facilities
    D. planning of resources

2. The director of planning of a local planning agency is *usually* responsible to the

    A. planning commission
    B. city council
    C. mayor
    D. city manager

3. The official map is subject to change ONLY by the

    A. planning commission
    B. city engineer
    C. legislative body
    D. mayor

4. An official map of a city is generally adopted by, and can ONLY be changed by action of the

    A. city engineer
    B. planning board
    C. legislative body
    D. zoning board of appeals

5. Zoning regulations are generally administered by the

    A. building department
    B. planning commission
    C. zoning board of appeals
    D. planning director

6. Logical extent of area which should be included in basic studies for a comprehensive city plan is

    A. entire residential area
    B. the neighborhood
    C. area bounded by city boundaries
    D. urban region

7. The safest angle (in degrees) for the intersection of two local streets is

    A. 45   B. 60   C. 90   D. 120

8. The city-beautiful movement is *usually* associated with work of

    A. L'Enfant   B. Burnham   C. Wright   D. Howard

9. The garden city movement is *usually* associated with

    A. Adams   B. Moses   C. Dahir   D. Howard

10. The power to permit variances to the zoning resolution is *usually* vested in the

    A. City Planning Commission
    B. Building Department
    C. City Council
    D. Board of Standards and Appeals

11. "Multiple Dwelling Law" is a

    A. federal law
    B. state law
    C. municipal ordinance
    D. law to protect landlords and hotels

12. The BEST map to use in planning a street layout for a new development is

    A. topographic
    B. planimetric
    C. photo-mosaic
    D. hydrographic chart

13. MAXIMUM auto traffic carrying capacity of a city street is attained at approximate speed of _____ M.P.H.

    A. 10-15   B. 15-25   C. 25-40   D. 40-55

14. A decelerating lane would *most likely* be used in conjunction with a

    A. bridge approach
    B. highway exit
    C. sharp curve on a highway
    D. steep grade on a highway

15. Use of curved streets in suburban development is *desirable* because it

    A. increases sight-distance for motorists
    B. makes a lot layout simpler
    C. forces motorists to reduce speed
    D. reduces surveying costs

16. The LEAST important requirement for a fire hydrant is

    A. accessibility
    B. artistic design
    C. frost proof
    D. mechanical reliability

17. In general, the *highest* tax return per acre of developed land is

    A. business
    B. industry
    C. apartments
    D. single family homes

18. The percentage of developed land area in a city normally taken up by the street system is about _____ %.

    A. 15   B. 25   C. 35   D. 45

19. The greatest amount of land in Manhattan is used for

    A. residences
    B. stores
    C. offices
    D. industry

20. The three "Greenbelt" towns in the United States after World War II were built by   20._____
    A. private capital
    B. the F.H.A.
    C. the Resettlement Administration
    D. the Department of Agriculture

KEY (CORRECT ANSWERS)

1.	A	11.	B
2.	A	12.	A
3.	C	13.	B
4.	C	14.	B
5.	A	15.	C
6.	D	16.	B
7.	C	17.	A
8.	B	18.	C
9.	D	19.	A
10.	D	20.	C

TEST 2

DIRECTIONS: Each question consists of a statement. You are to indicate whether the statement is TRUE (T) or FALSE (F). *PRINT THE LETTER OF THE CORRECT ANSWER IN THE SPACE AT THE RIGHT.*

1. In an *ideal plan,* radial express highways should lead to and through the downtown business center of a city. 1.____

2. In an ideal city plan for a large city, there should be circumferential transit lines NOT giving direct service to the central business district. 2.____

3. Modern limited access express highways for mixed traffic may appropriately be estimated, for purposes of adequacy of design, to have a practical capacity of 1200 to 1500 vehicles per lane per hour. 3.____

4. A city that is growing by constant decennial increments of total population would have a *straight-line* population curve when plotted on semi-logarithmic cross-section paper. 4.____

5. An infant mortality rate of 60 per 1000 live births per annum is representative of good health conditions in northeastern cities of the U.S. 5.____

6. A city which has 4 acres of land in use by industry, per 100 total resident population, would be considered highly industrialized. 6.____

7. The federal government, through the Department of Transportation, assists in financing new state highways within and outside corporate limits of cities. 7.____

8. The "riding habit" of Los Angeles would be expected to be *greater than* that of New York because of greater relative extent of use of private automobiles. 8.____

9. Because of lane friction and traffic weaving, a 4-lane one-way express roadway will NOT achieve a greater vehicle discharge per hour than a 3-lane one-way express roadway, all other design features being the same. 9.____

10. It is *good* practice to locate future playgrounds NOT more than one-quarter mile from any part of residential areas to be served. 10.____

11. An efficiently laid-out 18-hole golf course, under average topographic conditions, can be accomodated within 110 acres. 11.____

12. Elementary school sites of at least 5 acres are representative of good practice. 12.____

13. Senior high school sites of 25 to 40 acres are NOT considered extravagant or excessive under modern design standards. 13.____

14. Future school enrollments can be estimated by extrapolation of a curve showing percentage of total population which was enrolled in the school system in past years. 14.____

15. A "neighborhood unit" is a term used to embrace those planned residential area which constitute area of service of 1 junior high school. 15.____

16. "Company housing" is customarily used to describe colonies of dwelling units owned by an industrial corporation and rented individually to its employees. 16.____

17. In a *well-designed* residential subdivision, area of land in streets should NOT exceed 20 per cent of total area. 17._____

18. It is accepted *good* zoning practice to require large parking areas be screened from adjacent residential zones by landscaping. 18._____

19. "Floor area ratio" is quotient of ground floor area of a building divided by area of its lot. 19._____

20. The term "Unrestricted Districts" designates districts for which no use or area regulations or restrictions are provided by present zoning resolutions. 20._____

21. A rectangular block 200' x 810' has an area of about four acres. 21._____

22. Capacity of a highway *increases* directly with the speed. 22._____

23. A truck farm is prohibited in a residential district. 23._____

24. On a street with a crowned pavement, grade may be reduced to 0.0%. 24._____

25. Climate has NO effect on design of combined sewers. 25._____

26. Subgrade of a highway is the *lowest* grade ensuring adequate drainage. 26._____

27. Underdrainage results when inadequate storm sewers are provided. 27._____

28. Plans for bridges over navigable waterways require Army Corps of Engineers approval. 28._____

29. On a street with crossings at grade, the ONLY safety features added by widening a narrow median strip are further separation of opposing lanes of traffic and reduction of headlight glare. 29._____

30. In rural areas, need of sidewalks along highways depends on density of vehicular and pedestrian traffic and design speed of highway. 30._____

31. It is standard practice to design 2-lane highways with minimum sight distance such that overtaking and passing is possible in any section of the highway. 31._____

32. Widening pavements on curves is for *psychological* reasons ONLY. 32._____

33. An advantage of a concrete pavement is its high salvage value. 33._____

34. A *large* part of city planning consists of correction of mistakes. 34._____

35. Distribution of population is *usually* shown on a dot or density map. 35._____

36. A series of density maps showing population distribution at various dates is of NO more value to a city planner than the latest map of series. 36._____

37. In a *free* port, goods may be stored, repacked, manufactured, and reexported WITHOUT customs formalities. 37._____

38. Urban blight is due *solely* to lack of planning in original development. 38._____

39. The Chamber of Commerce of the United States recommends municipalities adopt building codes permitting use of any material or method of construction which meets minimum required standards of performance. 39.____

40. An accepted reliable method of estimating future population of small municipalities (under 10,000), for 5 years forward from the last census, involves extending past trend of birth rates, death rates, annual statistics of new dwelling units constructed, old dwelling units demolished, and average size of family. 40.____

KEY (CORRECT ANSWERS)

1. F	11. T	21. T	31. F
2. T	12. T	22. F	32. F
3. T	13. T	23. F	33. T
4. F	14. F	24. F	34. T
5. F	15. F	25. F	35. T
6. T	16. T	26. F	36. F
7. T	17. T	27. F	37. T
8. F	18. T	28. T	38. F
9. F	19. F	29. F	39. T
10. T	20. F	30. T	40. T

EXAMINATION SECTION
TEST 1

DIRECTIONS: Each question or incomplete statement is followed by several suggested answers or completions. Select the one that BEST answers the question or completes the statement. *PRINT THE LETTER OF THE CORRECT ANSWER IN THE SPACE AT THE RIGHT.*

1. The type of open space plaza built in conjunction with high rise buildings, now encouraged by city zoning laws, was first installed in the city of

    A. Lever House
    B. United Nations Headquarters
    C. Rockefeller Center
    D. Lincoln Center

    1.____

2. Of the following, *open space* in a residential site development is BEST insured by

    A. cluster design
    B. gridiron layout
    C. mixed building types
    D. density zoning

    2.____

3. Of the following statements concerning cast iron fronts built in the 19th century in the city, the one that is CORRECT is that they are

    A. still structurally sound
    B. being condemned for structural reasons
    C. not complex enough for preservation even though basically sound
    D. easily duplicated in the modern town houses.

    3.____

4. Of the following, the BEST example of the use of *eminent domain* is a

    A. planning board's reversal of a contested land use
    B. sale of public land for private development
    C. mayor authorizing the implementation of a zoning change
    D. tract of private land taken by the government for public purposes.

    4.____

5. Of the following measures of central tendency, the value of the variable which occurs MOST frequently is called the

    A. arithmetic mean
    B. harmonic mean
    C. median
    D. mode

    5.____

6. A MAJOR reason that industrial plants have been moving out of the city to the suburbs is that

    A. a cheap labor force is available
    B. union influence is eliminated
    C. plants can expand horizontally
    D. they will be closer to their market area

    6.____

7. The total floor area of a building divided by the lot area is called the

    A. net defensible space
    B. floor-area ratio
    C. rentable ratio
    D. open-space factor

    7.____

8. The State Multiple Dwelling Law defines a multiple dwelling as one that has _____ dwelling units.

   A. two or more
   B. three or more
   C. five or more
   D. over ten

9. Most zoning ordinances are NOT concerned with

   A. bulk regulations
   B. setbacks
   C. parking
   D. building materials

10. The site plan included in a set of drawings for a housing project will include all of the following EXCEPT

    A. existing structures
    B. easements and rights of way
    C. a plan of a typical floor
    D. boundary lines and distances

11. *Good* neighborhood planning should provide for

    A. the use of loop roads
    B. the use of cul-de-sacs
    C. a combination of loop roads and cul-de-sacs for ease of auto travel
    D. the separation of pedestrians and vehicles

12. An origin-destination survey is PRIMARILY made by

    A. educational planners
    B. market analysis expert
    C. transportation planners
    D. utility planners

13. Of the following, the concept of linear growth in urban areas refers PRIMARILY to growth of

    A. one type of dwelling only in each specific urban area
    B. the urban area along a major highway
    C. one-industry towns in a specific urban area
    D. urban areas in an orderly plan as opposed to haphazard development

14. In urban areas, it is BEST to locate mass transit facilities

    A. underground
    B. water's edge
    C. along major avenues
    D. so as to inter-connect high rise buildings

15. Of the following, the MAJOR contributing factor to the poor air quality in the city is

    A. smokestack emissions
    B. incinerators
    C. industrial waste
    D. auto exhaust emissions

16. The Municipal Loan Program was established to provide funds for

    A. new one-family housing
    B. low-cost housing in built-up areas
    C. altering and renovating old apartment buildings
    D. local planning boards

17. The towns of Radburn and Reston are *similar* to the extent that each

    A. has a man-made lake
    B. has a high rise housing building
    C. depends almost entirely on a cul-de-sac road system
    D. has mostly one-and two-story housing.

18. Of the following characteristics, the one MOST applicable to *zoning* is that zoning

    A. requires a sub-division layout for houses
    B. permits planned unit development in selected cases
    C. represents an attempt by local authorities to legally regulate use of land
    D. requires a typical topographic survey before enactment

19. Zoning laws are generally NOT concerned with

    A. architectural style
    B. building heights
    C. land use
    D. population density

20. In an average urban community, the percentage of land *usually* devoted to the street system is MOST NEARLY

    A. 5%
    B. 15%
    C. 35%
    D. 50%

21. The *railroad flat* obtained its name because it

    A. had all rooms in a straight line
    B. contained efficiency units
    C. was built with dimensions similar to Pullman train roomettes
    D. was originally built for railroad workers

22. A cul-de-sac is a

    A. circular driveway
    B. dead-end road
    C. highway interchange
    D. vehicular turning radius

23. MOST zoning ordinances prescribe minimum setbacks in order to provide

    A. adequate parking space
    B. maximum fire safety
    C. space for landscaping
    D. sufficient access, light, and air

24. The Critical Path Method

    A. is a form of scheduling operations against time periods and resources
    B. deals with program evaluation and actual costs
    C. concerns least cost estimating and scheduling
    D. is a tool to assure management that operations will proceed readily

25. According to the Building Code, every habitable room must be provided with natural light from windows. The sum of the areas of these windows must be at least equal to what minimum percentage of floor area of the room?

    A. 5%
    B. 10%
    C. 20%
    D. 25%

KEY (CORRECT ANSWERS)

1. C
2. A
3. A
4. D
5. D

6. C
7. B
8. B
9. D
10. C

11. D
12. C
13. B
14. A
15. D

16. C
17. D
18. C
19. A
20. C

21. A
22. B
23. D
24. A
25. B

TEST 2

DIRECTIONS: Each question or incomplete statement is followed by several suggested answers or completions. Select the one that BEST answers the question or completes the statement. *PRINT THE LETTER OF THE CORRECT ANSWER IN THE SPACE AT THE RIGHT.*

1. *Seed* money as it pertains to a new housing development is intended to   1.____

    A. broaden its scope
    B. restrict and channel the budget of the development
    C. encourage flexibilities and alternatives in the construction of development
    D. get it started

2. Incentive zoning is intended to compensate builders for   2.____

    A. inclusion of special projects in their proposal
    B. increasing the assessed valuation of property
    C. diversifying land use constraints
    D. addition of open space

3. A *performance bond* guarantees that   3.____

    A. a contractor will execute the terms of the contract
    B. the architect will oversee the completion of the contract
    C. the owner will pay the contractor upon the completion of his work
    D. the labor unions will enforce the proper completion of the contract

4. For buildings, the Zoning Resolution controls   4.____

    A. use, types, and bulk
    B. structure, materials, and egress
    C. heating, garbage, and superintendence
    D. landmark preservation, urban esthetics, and pollution

5. Of the following, the one that would contribute MOST toward reducing air pollution in an urban area is   5.____

    A. an increase in the number of parking garages
    B. the reduction of the number of cylinders in automobiles
    C. use of lower octane gasoline in automobiles
    D. an effective rapid transit system

6. PUD design refers to   6.____

    A. high rise housing
    B. housing spaced closely to net more open space
    C. less detached houses, more twinned and row houses
    D. roads around groups of houses

7. The one of the following that is the MOST common characteristic of an *educational park* in the United States is   7.____

    A. vertical high schools in large landscaped areas
    B. buildings for various levels of education in a related complex

11

C. various coeducational facilities at the high school level
D. high schools related to commerce and industry all on one site

8. An advantage of the *gridiron* system of urban layout is that it

   A. is most easily saleable by real estate brokers
   B. provides the most air and sunlight
   C. is easily adapted by surveyors
   D. makes use of normal topography

9. When parking is required in urban areas, the one of the following that is the MOST important benefit of creating this parking underground is

   A. the cost of the parking project is reduced
   B. air pollution in the area is reduced
   C. the land above may be used for other purposes
   D. cars are then hidden from sight

10. The MAJOR advantage of the use of the *superblock* is that it

    A. improves separation of vehicular and pedestrian circulation
    B. lends itself to modular expansion
    C. affords space to zone residential from industrial areas
    D. lends itself to flexible multi-zoning principles

11. The phrase *public right-of-way* refers to

    A. civil rights of individuals
    B. an easement
    C. a city street
    D. a public parking garage

12. A city-approved schedule of long-range construction projects extending over approximately a 6-year period is known as a(n)

    A. capital improvement program
    B. expense budget
    C. master plan
    D. flow chart

13. *Urban renewal* is the federal program PRIMARILY concerned with

    A. urban design
    B. advocate planning
    C. construction of new housing
    D. construction of new highways

14. As used in city planning, the number of persons per acre is referred to as the

    A. density
    B. use-ratio
    C. space-factor
    D. census

15. Of the following, the MOST efficient type of sanitary sewage disposal system is a

    A. cesspool
    B. public sewer
    C. septic tank
    D. storm drain

16. Full ownership of a dwelling unit and common ownership of community facilities is known as a

    A. cooperative
    B. rental unit
    C. condominium
    D. high rise development

17. The number of square feet in one acre of land is

    A. 22,100   B. 40,280   C. 43,560   D. 96,000

18. The MAIN function of a *collector street* is to

    A. conduct traffic from local streets to arterials
    B. provide access to abutting property
    C. provide open space between buildings
    D. carry heavy traffic

19. The *distinguishing* characteristic of a topographic map is its

    A. high and low water lines
    B. representation of terrestrial relief
    C. indications of the different types of soils
    D. illustrations of drainage areas

20. The *input-output* technique for urban economic analysis was originally designed for which one of the following economies?

    A. Municipal   B. National   C. State   D. Regional

21. The *cohort survival model* is one method of determining

    A. population
    B. death rate
    C. migration
    D. birth rate

22. Which one of the following items is DIRECTLY related to an urban land use survey?

    A. The classification system
    B. Physiographic features
    C. Flood area data
    D. The economic base

23. According to the requirements of the zoning ordinance, the basis of granting a variance is MOST often

    A. an economic loss
    B. physical hardship
    C. greater density
    D. change of use

24. Restrictive covenants or deed restrictions are MOST often considered to be

    A. local government regulations
    B. supplementary public controls
    C. subdivision plot requirements
    D. private contracts by property owners.

25. In the U.S. as a whole, when land is to be developed, the determination of street alignments would MOST frequently be made by which one of the following regulations?

   A. Zoning Ordinances
   B. Subdivision Regulations
   C. Health Department Rules
   D. Highway Department specifications

KEY (CORRECT ANSWERS)

1. D	11. C
2. A	12. A
3. A	13. C
4. A	14. A
5. D	15. B
6. B	16. C
7. B	17. C
8. C	18. A
9. C	19. B
10. A	20. B

21. A
22. D
23. B
24. D
25. B

EXAMINATION SECTION
TEST 1

DIRECTIONS: Each question or incomplete statement is followed by several suggested answers or completions. Select the one that BEST answers the question or completes the statement. *PRINT THE LETTER OF THE CORRECT ANSWER IN THE SPACE AT THE RIGHT.*

1. The type of open space plaza built in conjunction with high rise buildings, now encouraged by city zoning laws, was first installed in the city of

   A. Lever House
   B. United Nations Headquarters
   C. Rockefeller Center
   D. Lincoln Center

2. Of the following, *open space* in a residential site development is BEST insured by

   A. cluster design
   B. gridiron layout
   C. mixed building types
   D. density zoning

3. Of the following statements concerning cast iron fronts built in the 19th century in the city, the one that is CORRECT is that they are

   A. still structurally sound
   B. being condemned for structural reasons
   C. not complex enough for preservation even though basically sound
   D. easily duplicated in the modern town houses.

4. Of the following, the BEST example of the use of *eminent domain* is a

   A. planning board's reversal of a contested land use
   B. sale of public land for private development
   C. mayor authorizing the implementation of a zoning change
   D. tract of private land taken by the government for public purposes.

5. Of the following measures of central tendency, the value of the variable which occurs MOST frequently is called the

   A. arithmetic mean
   B. harmonic mean
   C. median
   D. mode

6. A MAJOR reason that industrial plants have been moving out of the city to the suburbs is that

   A. a cheap labor force is available
   B. union influence is eliminated
   C. plants can expand horizontally
   D. they will be closer to their market area

7. The total floor area of a building divided by the lot area is called the

   A. net defensible space
   B. floor-area ratio
   C. rentable ratio
   D. open-space factor

8. The State Multiple Dwelling Law defines a multiple dwelling as one that has _____ dwelling units.

   A. two or more
   B. three or more
   C. five or more
   D. over ten

9. Most zoning ordinances are NOT concerned with

   A. bulk regulations
   B. setbacks
   C. parking
   D. building materials

10. The site plan included in a set of drawings for a housing project will include all of the following EXCEPT

    A. existing structures
    B. easements and rights of way
    C. a plan of a typical floor
    D. boundary lines and distances

11. *Good* neighborhood planning should provide for

    A. the use of loop roads
    B. the use of cul-de-sacs
    C. a combination of loop roads and cul-de-sacs for ease of auto travel
    D. the separation of pedestrians and vehicles

12. An origin-destination survey is PRIMARILY made by

    A. educational planners
    B. market analysis expert
    C. transportation planners
    D. utility planners

13. Of the following, the concept of linear growth in urban areas refers PRIMARILY to growth of

    A. one type of dwelling only in each specific urban area
    B. the urban area along a major highway
    C. one-industry towns in a specific urban area
    D. urban areas in an orderly plan as opposed to haphazard development

14. In urban areas, it is BEST to locate mass transit facilities

    A. underground
    B. water's edge
    C. along major avenues
    D. so as to inter-connect high rise buildings

15. Of the following, the MAJOR contributing factor to the poor air quality in the city is

    A. smokestack emissions
    B. incinerators
    C. industrial waste
    D. auto exhaust emissions

16. The Municipal Loan Program was established to provide funds for

    A. new one-family housing
    B. low-cost housing in built-up areas
    C. altering and renovating old apartment buildings
    D. local planning boards

17. The towns of Radburn and Reston are *similar* to the extent that each 17.____

    A. has a man-made lake
    B. has a high rise housing building
    C. depends almost entirely on a cul-de-sac road system
    D. has mostly one-and two-story housing.

18. Of the following characteristics, the one MOST applicable to *zoning* is that zoning 18.____

    A. requires a sub-division layout for houses
    B. permits planned unit development in selected cases
    C. represents an attempt by local authorities to legally regulate use of land
    D. requires a typical topographic survey before enactment

19. Zoning laws are generally NOT concerned with 19.____

    A. architectural style   B. building heights
    C. land use   D. population density

20. In an average urban community, the percentage of land *usually* devoted to the street system is MOST NEARLY 20.____

    A. 5%   B. 15%   C. 35%   D. 50%

21. The *railroad flat* obtained its name because it 21.____

    A. had all rooms in a straight line
    B. contained efficiency units
    C. was built with dimensions similar to Pullman train roomettes
    D. was originally built for railroad workers

22. A cul-de-sac is a 22.____

    A. circular driveway   B. dead-end road
    C. highway interchange   D. vehicular turning radius

23. MOST zoning ordinances prescribe minimum setbacks in order to provide 23.____

    A. adequate parking space
    B. maximum fire safety
    C. space for landscaping
    D. sufficient access, light, and air

24. The Critical Path Method 24.____

    A. is a form of scheduling operations against time periods and resources
    B. deals with program evaluation and actual costs
    C. concerns least cost estimating and scheduling
    D. is a tool to assure management that operations will proceed readily

25. According to the Building Code, every habitable room must be provided with natural light from windows. The sum of the areas of these windows must be at least equal to what minimum percentage of floor area of the room? 25.____

    A. 5%   B. 10%   C. 20%   D. 25%

KEY (CORRECT ANSWERS)

1.	C	11.	D
2.	A	12.	C
3.	A	13.	B
4.	D	14.	A
5.	D	15.	D
6.	C	16.	C
7.	B	17.	D
8.	B	18.	C
9.	D	19.	A
10.	C	20.	C

21. A
22. B
23. D
24. A
25. B

TEST 2

DIRECTIONS: Each question or incomplete statement is followed by several suggested answers or completions. Select the one that BEST answers the question or completes the statement. *PRINT THE LETTER OF THE CORRECT ANSWER IN THE SPACE AT THE RIGHT.*

1. *Seed* money as it pertains to a new housing development is intended to 1.____

    A. broaden its scope
    B. restrict and channel the budget of the development
    C. encourage flexibilities and alternatives in the construction of development
    D. get it started

2. Incentive zoning is intended to compensate builders for 2.____

    A. inclusion of special projects in their proposal
    B. increasing the assessed valuation of property
    C. diversifying land use constraints
    D. addition of open space

3. A *performance bond* guarantees that 3.____

    A. a contractor will execute the terms of the contract
    B. the architect will oversee the completion of the contract
    C. the owner will pay the contractor upon the completion of his work
    D. the labor unions will enforce the proper completion of the contract

4. For buildings, the Zoning Resolution controls 4.____

    A. use, types, and bulk
    B. structure, materials, and egress
    C. heating, garbage, and superintendence
    D. landmark preservation, urban esthetics, and pollution

5. Of the following, the one that would contribute MOST toward reducing air pollution in an urban area is 5.____

    A. an increase in the number of parking garages
    B. the reduction of the number of cylinders in automobiles
    C. use of lower octane gasoline in automobiles
    D. an effective rapid transit system

6. PUD design refers to 6.____

    A. high rise housing
    B. housing spaced closely to net more open space
    C. less detached houses, more twinned and row houses
    D. roads around groups of houses

7. The one of the following that is the MOST common characteristic of an *educational park* in the United States is 7.____

    A. vertical high schools in large landscaped areas
    B. buildings for various levels of education in a related complex

19

C. various coeducational facilities at the high school level
D. high schools related to commerce and industry all on one site

8. An advantage of the *gridiron* system of urban layout is that it

   A. is most easily saleable by real estate brokers
   B. provides the most air and sunlight
   C. is easily adapted by surveyors
   D. makes use of normal topography

9. When parking is required in urban areas, the one of the following that is the MOST important benefit of creating this parking underground is

   A. the cost of the parking project is reduced
   B. air pollution in the area is reduced
   C. the land above may be used for other purposes
   D. cars are then hidden from sight

10. The MAJOR advantage of the use of the *superblock* is that it

    A. improves separation of vehicular and pedestrian circulation
    B. lends itself to modular expansion
    C. affords space to zone residential from industrial areas
    D. lends itself to flexible multi-zoning principles

11. The phrase *public right-of-way* refers to

    A. civil rights of individuals
    B. an easement
    C. a city street
    D. a public parking garage

12. A city-approved schedule of long-range construction projects extending over approximately a 6-year period is known as a(n)

    A. capital improvement program
    B. expense budget
    C. master plan
    D. flow chart

13. *Urban renewal* is the federal program PRIMARILY concerned with

    A. urban design
    B. advocate planning
    C. construction of new housing
    D. construction of new highways

14. As used in city planning, the number of persons per acre is referred to as the

    A. density
    B. use-ratio
    C. space-factor
    D. census

15. Of the following, the MOST efficient type of sanitary sewage disposal system is a

    A. cesspool
    B. public sewer
    C. septic tank
    D. storm drain

16. Full ownership of a dwelling unit and common ownership of community facilities is known as a

    A. cooperative
    B. rental unit
    C. condominium
    D. high rise development

17. The number of square feet in one acre of land is

    A. 22,100   B. 40,280   C. 43,560   D. 96,000

18. The MAIN function of a *collector street* is to

    A. conduct traffic from local streets to arterials
    B. provide access to abutting property
    C. provide open space between buildings
    D. carry heavy traffic

19. The *distinguishing* characteristic of a topographic map is its

    A. high and low water lines
    B. representation of terrestrial relief
    C. indications of the different types of soils
    D. illustrations of drainage areas

20. The *input-output* technique for urban economic analysis was originally designed for which one of the following economies?

    A. Municipal   B. National   C. State   D. Regional

21. The *cohort survival model* is one method of determining

    A. population
    B. death rate
    C. migration
    D. birth rate

22. Which one of the following items is DIRECTLY related to an urban land use survey?

    A. The classification system
    B. Physiographic features
    C. Flood area data
    D. The economic base

23. According to the requirements of the zoning ordinance, the basis of granting a variance is MOST often

    A. an economic loss
    B. physical hardship
    C. greater density
    D. change of use

24. Restrictive covenants or deed restrictions are MOST often considered to be

    A. local government regulations
    B. supplementary public controls
    C. subdivision plot requirements
    D. private contracts by property owners.

25. In the U.S. as a whole, when land is to be developed, the determination of street alignments would MOST frequently be made by which one of the following regulations?

    A. Zoning Ordinances
    B. Subdivision Regulations
    C. Health Department Rules
    D. Highway Department specifications

25.____

KEY (CORRECT ANSWERS)

1.	D	11.	C
2.	A	12.	A
3.	A	13.	C
4.	A	14.	A
5.	D	15.	B
6.	B	16.	C
7.	B	17.	C
8.	C	18.	A
9.	C	19.	B
10.	A	20.	B

21.	A
22.	D
23.	B
24.	D
25.	B

EXAMINATION SECTION
TEST 1

DIRECTIONS: Each question or incomplete statement is followed by several suggested, answers or completions. Select the one that BEST answers the question or completes the statement. *PRINT THE LETTER OF THE CORRECT ANSWER IN THE SPACE AT THE RIGHT.*

1. The authority to establish zoning ordinances by a community comes from

   A. the police power of the state
   B. local determination
   C. the federal government
   D. implied powers of the community

   1.____

2. On a land use map, the standard color used to designate residential use is

   A. green   B. blue   C. purple   D. yellow

   2.____

3. In population analysis, a population pyramid indicates

   A. male and female age groupings
   B. total population projections
   C. fertility ratios
   D. educational achievements

   3.____

4. The determination of a standard metropolitan statistical area is established by

   A. local considerations
   B. regional agencies
   C. the U.S. Census Bureau
   D. state agencies

   4.____

5. The population census of the United States is taken every _____ years.

   A. 2   B. 4   C. 5   D. 10

   5.____

6. There are strong indications that planning agencies are developing a new approach to the traditional methods of city planning.
   This new approach is called

   A. advocacy planning
   B. long-range physical planning
   C. community development
   D. policies planning

   6.____

7. A key element of a comprehensive plan for a community is the

   A. zoning ordinance
   B. land use plan
   C. official map
   D. subdivision regulation

   7.____

8. The official map of a community is a document that

   A. shows population projections and educational trends
   B. pinpoints the location of future streets and other public facilities
   C. identifies capital improvements and budgets
   D. indicates all community facilities

   8.____

9. During the past decade, planning programs generally have become increasingly concerned with which one of the following?

   A. Long-range physical design
   B. Highway locations
   C. Social welfare
   D. Natural resources

10. The city planning process encompasses several basic phases. Which one of the following phases would NOT be considered typical?

    A. Cost-benefit analysis
    B. Goal formulation
    C. Data collection and research
    D. Plan preparation and programming

11. The MOST common use of easements in new housing subdivisions is for

    A. air rights   B. utilities
    C. open space   D. absorption fields

12. The phrase *non-complying use* relates to which one of the following regulations?

    A. Zoning Ordinance   B. Building Code
    C. Subdivision regulations D. Health Code

13. Performance standards are generally associated with which one of the following types of zoning districts?

    A. Residential   B. Commercial
    C. Manufacturing   D. Flood plain

14. The PRIMARY goal of cluster-type development is to

    A. increase population density
    B. insure open space
    C. discourage rapid development
    D. bypass zoning requirements

15. Which of the following is MOST closely related to the land-use intensity standards developed by the Federal Housing Administration?

    A. Quality of housing   B. Planned unit development
    C. Low-cost housing   D. Land management policy

16. If the density of a residential subdivision is 8 dwelling units per acre, then the average size lot should be APPROXIMATELY

    A. 25 ft. x 100 ft.   B. 55 ft. x 100 ft.
    C. 100 ft. x 100 ft.   D. 200 ft. x 200 ft.

17. In planning the open parking area for community facilities, the amount of space allocated per care should be APPROXIMATELY _____ sq.ft.

    A. 150   B. 300   C. 600   D. 800

18. Which of the following facilities would be MOST appropriate on the roof of a building? 18.____

    A. Stolport B. Heliport
    C. Airport D. Cargo port

19. Sanitary landfill is a method of 19.____

    A. sewage disposal B. composting
    C. incineration D. refuse disposal

20. Which of the following is NOT considered to be an air pollutant by the Environmental Protection Agency? 20.____

    A. Nitrates B. Sulfur oxides
    C. Carbon monoxide D. Hydrocarbons

21. Which of the following recreation facilities is NOT considered a typical neighborhood facility? 21.____

    A. Tot lot B. Playground
    C. Wading pool D. Playfield

22. Which of the following methods would be the MOST accurate in making a population projection for a small community? 22.____

    A. Migration and natural increase
    B. Apportionment and voting records
    C. School enrollment and housing starts
    D. Geometric extrapolation

23. When a planning map is to be reproduced to different sizes, the map scale should be expressed 23.____

    A. mathematically B. in graphic form
    C. in feet and inches D. by metes and bounds

24. The one of the following characteristics which is NOT typical of new industrial parks is 24.____

    A. off-street loading B. extensive landscaping
    C. employee parking D. 2-story structures

25. A greenbelt surrounding a community can be used for many activities. The one of the following activities LEAST appropriate for greenbelt use is 25.____

    A. farming B. recreation
    C. local shopping D. flood plain control

KEY (CORRECT ANSWERS)

1.	A	11.	B
2.	D	12.	A
3.	A	13.	C
4.	C	14.	B
5.	D	15.	B
6.	D	16.	B
7.	B	17.	B
8.	B	18.	B
9.	C	19.	D
10.	A	20.	A

21. D
22. A
23. B
24. D
25. C

TEST 2

DIRECTIONS: Each question or incomplete statement is followed by several suggested answers or completions. Select the one that BEST answers the question or completes the statement. *PRINT THE LETTER OF THE CORRECT ANSWER IN THE SPACE AT THE RIGHT.*

1. The *neighborhood unit* concept does NOT provide for

   A. elementary schools B. playgrounds
   C. local shopping D. industrial development

   1.____

2. Which of the following areas is LEAST likely to be considered part of social welfare planning?

   A. Urban design B. Education
   C. Health D. Anti-poverty

   2.____

3. Both the census of business and the census of manufacturing compiled by the U.S. Bureau of the Census are made every _____ years.

   A. three B. five C. seven D. ten

   3.____

4. The MOST frequently used governmental source for topographical maps is the U.S.

   A. Department of Agriculture
   B. Geological Survey
   C. Department of Housing and Urban Development
   D. Coast Guard

   4.____

5. The importance of assessed valuation of land and buildings to a community is to

   A. establish school taxes
   B. establish property taxes
   C. determine tax exemptions
   D. determine land uses

   5.____

6. Of the following countries, the MOST extensive progress in establishing new towns during the 20th century has taken place in

   A. the United States B. France
   C. Italy D. England

   6.____

7. A street classification system is PRIMARILY used for street

   A. naming B. construction
   C. differentiation D. location

   7.____

8. The *Greenbelt* towns were a product of the

   A. city beautiful movement
   B. garden city movement
   C. atomic energy commission
   D. resettlement administration

   8.____

27

9. The apportionment method of population projection is concerned PRIMARILY with   9.____

   A. migration B. natural increase
   C. large geographic areas D. birth rate

10. Under ideal conditions, which type of parking arrangement should yield the MOST parking spaces?   10.____

    A. Parallel   B. 45°   C. 60°   D. 90°

11. A MAJOR disadvantage of a depressed highway through a built-up area as compared to a highway on grade is its   11.____

    A. poor appearance
    B. inadequate width of right-of-way
    C. lack of access
    D. noise generation

12. The customary test made to determine the ability of a soil to drain off liquids, such as those discharged by a cesspool, is known as the _____ test.   12.____

    A. percolation B. absorption
    C. drainage D. sump

13. The Mitchell-Lama Housing Law was originally intended to assist the construction of   13.____

    A. low-income housing
    B. middle-income housing
    C. suburban residential projects
    D. housing for mixed racial communities

14. A community will MOST frequently acquire the development rights of existing farm land in order to   14.____

    A. protect land values
    B. provide sites for public projects
    C. insure open space
    D. develop a land bank

15. In recent years, local participation in the city planning process has *substantially* increased because of the   15.____

    A. establishment of local school boards
    B. high crime rate in the streets
    C. emergence of private citizen organizations
    D. establishment of community planning boards

16. A unique feature of the State Urban Development Corporation when first established was that it   16.____

    A. was an autonomous organization
    B. was not required to conform to local zoning regulations
    C. could only build housing when invited by local communities
    D. used only private funds for its projects

17. The concept of *defensible space* has recently emerged to help fight crime in urban areas. The principle of *defensible space* is that public areas should be

    A. completely enclosed
    B. eliminated
    C. placed adjacent to areas of activity
    D. patroled by volunteer citizen groups

    17.____

18. Of the following, the MAJOR planning implication of a 3-bedroom dwelling unit as compared to a 1-bedroom dwelling unit is that

    A. the family with the larger dwelling unit has more income
    B. with larger dwelling units there will be fewer municipal services necessary
    C. more children will be enrolled in school
    D. smaller dwelling units are cheaper to build than larger units

    18.____

19. A landscaped buffer strip is MOST appropriately placed between which of the following land uses?

    A. Light and heavy manufacturing
    B. Residential and commercial
    C. Commercial and manufacturing
    D. Residential of low density and residential of high density

    19.____

20. The employment trend in the city over the past 20 years has shown that

    A. *both* white collar and blue collar jobs have increased
    B. *both* white collar and blue collar jobs have decreased
    C. *only* white collar jobs have decreased
    D. *only* blue collar jobs have decreased

    20.____

21. For traffic safety, the BEST angle between two intersecting streets is

    A. 15   B. 30   C. 45   D. 90

    21.____

22. In the city, the system used by the tax department to identify property is by

    A. house numbers   B. zoning maps
    C. block and lot numbers   D. the official city map

    22.____

23. The name of the report by which the U.S. Environmental Protection Agency establishes the effect of a proposed project on the environment is called the

    A. input-output analysis   B. economic base study
    C. ambient air study   D. impact statement

    23.____

24. Planners recommend that utility lines be located underground because utility lines built this way are

    A. cheaper to construct
    B. not required to follow street alignments
    C. aesthetically more attractive
    D. more efficient

    24.____

25. *Scatter-site* housing means that the housing will be
   A. located in all use districts
   B. built with large areas of recreation space between buildings
   C. of different heights on each site
   D. built on small, by-passed sites in built-up areas

KEY (CORRECT ANSWERS)

1.	D	11.	C
2.	A	12.	A
3.	B	13.	B
4.	B	14.	C
5.	B	15.	D
6.	D	16.	B
7.	C	17.	C
8.	D	18.	C
9.	C	19.	B
10.	D	20.	D

21. D
22. C
23. D
24. C
25. D

EXAMINATION SECTION
TEST 1

DIRECTIONS: Each question or incomplete statement is followed by several suggested answers or completions. Select the one that BEST answers the question or completes the statement. *PRINT THE LETTER OF THE CORRECT ANSWER IN THE SPACE AT THE RIGHT.*

1. The Model Cities program, which was authorized by the *Demonstration Cities and Metropolitan Development Act* was designed to

    A. help selected areas plan, administer, and carry out coordinated physical and social programs to improve the environment
    B. aid non-profit organizations to develop and demonstrate new ways of providing housing for low-income families
    C. encourage architects and builders to devise new large-scale construction techniques
    D. offer an alternative to usual urban renewal procedures through funding specific renewal activities on a yearly basis

2. The MAJOR purpose of the capital budgeting process in local government is to

    A. provide operating funds for the various departments
    B. centralize budget decision power in the executive branch
    C. centralize budget decision power in the Council
    D. establish a rational system of priorities for construction

3. The economic base of a community is

    A. the number of wealthy people with annual earnings in excess of $100,000 per year as a ratio to the total population
    B. the percentage of factory employed residents as a ratio of the total work force
    C. the productive industries located within the boundaries of a community
    D. those activities which provide the basic employment and income on which the rest of the local economy depends

4. One of the reasons for the creation of *superagencies* within city government was to

    A. create agencies that would serve as liaisons between the mayor's office and the community
    B. decentralize some of the functions for which the old agencies formerly had responsibility
    C. make each agency autonomous
    D. eliminate duplication of activities among different agencies

5. The word *autonomy* means

    A. automatic
    B. disregard of externals
    C. unlimited power or authority
    D. independent, self-governing

6. De facto, as in de facto segregation, means 6._____

   A. by right, in accordance with law
   B. actual
   C. disguised
   D. unintentional

7. American cities gain their legal powers from 7._____

   A. the Federal government
   B. the State government
   C. the United States Constitution
   D. common law

8. In an average urban area, the one of the following land uses that would account for the LARGEST percentage of land is 8._____

   A. residences   B. streets
   C. business and industry   D. public and semi-public uses

9. A cul-de-sac street is a 9._____

   A. dead-end street terminating in a circular turn-around
   B. loop street branching off from a collector street
   C. narrow street which has become congested as the result of commercial development
   D. gridiron street on which through traffic is prohibited

10. In the city, the capital budget is initially prepared by the 10._____

    A. city council   B. comptroller
    C. city planning commission   D. budget director

11. Reasonably well-to-do residential communities have joined the search for non-residential taxpayers but have shown LEAST inclination to plan for 11._____

    A. the necessary public utilities
    B. adequate access to the sites
    C. housing the workers
    D. the Budget Director

12. The GREATEST percentage of the daytime population of the business center of the city arrives by 12._____

    A. railroad   B. subway
    C. bus   D. passenger car

13. The LARGEST single public expenditure in most cities and suburbs in the State is for 13._____

    A. schools and education
    B. highways
    C. hospitals and health facilities
    D. police protection

14. The legal basis of zoning is

    A. the police power
    B. the power to levy taxes
    C. the Federal Constitution
    D. a special act of Congress

    14._____

15. A drug used in addiction programs as a substitute for heroin is

    A. benzedrine   B. librium
    C. methadone   D. methanimine

    15._____

16. The STOLcraft is a(n)

    A. high speed hydrofoil proposed as an alternative to the use of the ferry
    B. vehicle which travels just above the surface of either land or water on a cushion of air
    C. airplane intended for short distance trips between city centers
    D. cargo ship for containerized freight

    16._____

Questions 17-21.

DIRECTIONS: Questions 17 through 21 are to be answered on the basis of the following information.

FLOOR AREA

Floor area is the sum of the gross areas of the several floors of a building or buildings, measured from the exterior faces of exterior walls or from the center lines of walls separating two buildings.

FLOOR AREA RATIO

Floor area ratio is the total floor area on a zoning lot, divided by the lot area of that zoning lot. (For example, a building containing 20,000 square feet of floor area on a zoning lot of 10,000 square feet has a floor area ratio of 2.0.) Expressed as a formula:

$$FAR = \frac{Floor\ Area}{Lot\ Area}$$

OPEN SPACE RATIO

The *open space ratio* of a zoning lot is the number of square feet of open space on the zoning lot, expressed as a percentage of the floor area on that zoning lot. (For example, if for a particular building an open space ratio of 20 is required, 20,000 square feet of floor area in the building would necessitate 4,000 square feet of open space on the zoning lot upon which the building stands, or, if 6,000 square feet of lot area were in open space, 30,000 square feet of floor area could be in the building on that zoning lot.) Each square foot of open space per 100 square feet of floor area is referred to as one point.

Expressed as a formula:

$$OSR = \frac{100 \times open\ space}{Floor\ Area}$$

17. If a building can be built with a maximum floor area ratio (FAR) of 10.0, this means   17.____
    A. the building can have a maximum of ten stories
    B. the maximum ratio of gross square feet of floor area to area of the first floor is 10:1
    C. that open space on the zoning lot must be provided in an amount equal to ten percent of the total floor area of the building
    D. the maximum ratio of gross square feet of floor area to lot area is 10:1

18. If the open space ratio of a particular building is 18.5 and the actual amount of open space is 13,550 square feet, the floor area of the building must be MOST NEARLY   18.____

    A. 250,675   B. 73,243   C. 28,170   D. 79,027

19. Given: A housing site of 43,560 square feet.   19.____
    At an FAR of 3.33, the allowable total floor area of a proposed building would be MOST NEARLY

    A. 30,736   B. 484,482   C. 48,448   D. 145,055

20. Given: A housing site of 43,560 square feet.   20.____
    At an FAR of 2.94 and an open space ratio of 24.0, how much open space must be provided?

    A. 30,736   B. 10,454   C. 14,816   D. 18,150

21. Given: A housing site of 43,560 square feet.   21.____
    If a proposed building on this site were to have 122,839 gross square feet of floor space, what would the FAR be?

    A. 10.0
    B. 25.5
    C. 2.82
    D. Cannot be determined from data given

Questions 22-24.

DIRECTIONS: Questions 22 through 24 are to be answered on the basis of the following table.

The age characteristics of the total population in a certain neighborhood are as follows:

Age	Number of People
3	2
5	4
12	3
18	3
20	1
21	3
22	4
50	2
56	1
72	2

22. The mean age of the population in the neighborhood described above is MOST NEARLY   22.____

    A. 15   B. 19   C. 23   D. 27

23. The median age of the population in the neighborhood described above is MOST   23.____
    NEARLY

    A. 15   B. 20   C. 25   D. 30

24. The percentage of the population over age 65 in the neighborhood described above is   24.____
    MOST NEARLY

    A. 2   B. 4   C. 6   D. 8

25.   25.____

    [Diagram: A large rectangle containing a smaller rectangle labeled "TOWER"; width of large rectangle = 800 ft]

    Assume that the above drawing has been made to scale. The total gross floor area of
    the 20-story tower is, in square feet, MOST NEARLY

    A. 200,000   B. 100,000   C. 1,000   D. 50,000

KEY (CORRECT ANSWERS)

1.	A	11.	C
2.	D	12.	B
3.	D	13.	A
4.	D	14.	A
5.	D	15.	C
6.	B	16.	C
7.	B	17.	D
8.	A	18.	B
9.	A	19.	D
10.	C	20.	A

21. C
22. C
23. B
24. D
25. A

TEST 2

DIRECTIONS: Each question or incomplete statement is followed by several suggested answers or completions. Select the one that BEST answers the question or completes the statement. *PRINT THE LETTER OF THE CORRECT ANSWER IN THE SPACE AT THE RIGHT.*

1. In the city, the body that is responsible for choosing the specific location of sites for public improvement is the

    A. city planning commission
    B. department of public works
    C. site selection board
    D. fine arts commission

    1.____

2. Publicly-sponsored Early Childhood programs in the city do NOT include

    A. Family Day Care
    B. Headstart Program
    C. playschools for 2- and 3-year olds
    D. pre-kindergarten in elementary schools

    2.____

3. The one of the following that is NOT a current method of controlling pollution is the

    A. requirement that incinerators in the city be upgraded
    B. project for recycling waste paper and aluminum goods for re-use
    C. sale of non-leaded gasoline for automobiles
    D. conversion of all combined sewers in the city to separate sanitary and storm sewers

    3.____

4. In general, the MOST accurate 5-year projection of population can be made for the

    A. nation   B. metropolitan area
    C. inner city   D. neighborhood

    4.____

5. The type of area in which the GREATEST percentage increase in population occurred between 1960 and 1980 was in the

    A. central cities   B. suburban rings
    C. rural non-farm areas D. rural farm areas

    5.____

6. The one of the following that should NOT be included in a community planning study undertaken by a city planning department is

    A. a survey of how land is used in the area
    B. compilation of data on school utilization
    C. determination of rent levels in the area
    D. renovation of an old building at rents suitable for low-income people

    6.____

7. The one of the following men who had a role in laying out cities along the formal lines of the *City Beautiful* movement was

    A. Rexford Tugwell   B. Daniel Burnham
    C. Clarence Stein   D. Frank Lloyd Wright

    7.____

8. A key factor leading to the development of suburban growth in recent decades is 8.____

   A. a series of regional government compacts
   B. the large increase in automobile ownership
   C. the drying up of immigration
   D. the gradual shifting of some shopping and employment from the center of the city to the outskirts

9. A controlled aerial mosaic photograph would be LEAST useful in which of the following types of planning work? 9.____

   A. Land use study of undeveloped land
   B. Review of subdivision plats
   C. Study of proposed highway locations
   D. Building condition study of CBD

10. The MAJOR function of the city community planning boards is 10.____

    A. to prepare capital and expense budgets for community planning districts
    B. to advise the county executives and city agencies on planning issues
    C. as an umbrella organization for local poverty groups
    D. to provide technical planning help to local community groups

11. Special revenue sharing is intended to 11.____

    A. be available only for cities of over 1 million population
    B. be available for general purpose use, to be determined by the cities
    C. replace money previously distributed to cities for categorical grants
    D. in all instances be passed from the state to the city

12. The city's water pollution control plants are being upgraded to _____ treatment which removes _____. 12.____

    A. primary; "approximately" 65% of pollutants
    B. secondary; approximately 90% of pollutants
    C. tertiary; approximately 99% of pollutants
    D. desalination; all the mineral matter

13. *Turnkey* housing refers to 13.____

    A. a method of housing construction whereby a private developer finances and constructs the housing to the city's standards and the housing is then purchased by the city
    B. the conversion of old-law housing to co-op housing in moderate rent areas, including rent subsidies for low-income families
    C. brownstone renovation with no public subsidy in historic districts where the design must be approved by the landmarks commission
    D. a form of mixing housing with commercial or industrial space, as in the incentive zoning amendment

14. The Planned-Unit Development is a provision of the city zoning resolution which   14.____

    A. provides for industrial development on the outskirts of the city
    B. requires the building of schools, community centers, and shopping facilities as part of a large residential development
    C. permits housing to be built close together in clusters, leaving substantial land areas in their natural state as common open spaces
    D. provides a means of constructing off-street parking facilities in high density residential neighborhoods

15. The official map differs from the master plan in that it   15.____

    A. deals only with proposed streets as they relate to existing streets
    B. includes a detailed engineering design for the existing and proposed street system
    C. is an accurate description of the location of public improvements existing and proposed
    D. is tied directly to the Capital Budget and Improvement Program

16. According to the zoning resolution, a legal non-conforming use in zoning is one established   16.____

    A. prior to the adoption of the ordinance provision prohibiting it
    B. by a special exception permit issued by the planning commission
    C. by a variance issued by the board of standards and appeals
    D. for many years despite the prohibition in the ordinance and which had not been proceeded against

17. The formula for financing interstate highways under state and Federal law provides that the government of the city shall pay what percent of the cost of highway construction?   17.____

    A. 100%   B. 90%   C. 40%   D. 0%

18. The one of the following statements that MOST NEARLY expresses the city's long-term program in regard to arterial highways is to   18.____

    A. provide many routes throughout the city in order to minimize travel time from all points
    B. provide quick vehicular access from the business center to the suburbs
    C. build up bypass routes to discourage traffic from entering the business center
    D. build up the highway network in the outer boroughs and to landbank land in the business center for future through routes

19. The city planning commission   19.____

    A. consists of lifetime members, who annually elect a chairman
    B. administers the zoning resolution and hears appeals for variances
    C. prepares the annual 5-year capital improvement plan
    D. prepares the architectural designs for all public buildings, except schools

20. The feature of the city zoning resolution before 1961 which gave the city's skyscrapers their MOST distinctive architectural character was its

    A. height bonus for added setbacks
    B. rear yard provisions
    C. off-street parking and loading requirements
    D. density restrictions

KEY (CORRECT ANSWERS)

1.	C	11.	C
2.	C	12.	B
3.	D	13.	A
4.	A	14.	C
5.	B	15.	A
6.	D	16.	A
7.	B	17.	D
8.	B	18.	C
9.	D	19.	C
10.	B	20.	A

TEST 3

DIRECTIONS: Each question or incomplete statement is followed by several suggested answers or completions. Select the one that BEST answers the question or completes the statement. *PRINT THE LETTER OF THE CORRECT ANSWER IN THE SPACE AT THE RIGHT.*

Questions 1-3.

DIRECTIONS: Questions 1 through 3, inclusive, are to be answered in accordance with the following paragraphs.

Into the nine square miles that make up Manhattan's business districts, about two million people travel each weekday to go to work — the equivalent of the combined populations of Boston, Baltimore, and Cincinnati. Some 140,000 drive there in cars, 200,000 take buses, and 100,000 ride the commuter railroads. The great majority, however, go by subway — approximately 1.4 million people.

It is some ride. The last major improvement in the subway system was completed in 1935. The subways are dirty and noisy. Many local lines operate well beneath capacity; but many express lines are strained way beyond capacity in particular, the lines to Manhattan, now overloaded by 39,000 passengers during peak hours.

But for all its discomforts, the subway system is inherently a far more efficient way of moving people than automobiles and highways. Making this system faster, more convenient, and more comfortable for people must be the core of the city's transportation effort.

1. The CENTRAL point of the above text is that	1.____

   A. the equivalent of the combined populations of Boston, Baltimore, and Cincinnati commute into Manhattan's business district each weekday
   B. the improvement of the subway system is the key to the solution of moving people efficiently in and out of Manhattan's business district
   C. the subways are dirty and noisy, resulting in a terrible ride
   D. we should increase the ability of people to get in and out of Manhattan by cars, subways, and commuter railroads in order to ease the load from the subways

2. In accordance with the above paragraphs, 1.4 million people commute by subway and	2.____
   _____ by other mass transportation means.

   A. 200,000   B. 100,000   C. 440,000   D. 300,000

3. From the information given in the above paragraphs, one could logically conclude that,	3.____
   next to the subways, the transportation system that carries the LARGEST number of passengers is (the)

   A. railroads   B. cars
   C. buses   D. local lines

Questions 4-6.

DIRECTIONS: Questions 4 through 6, inclusive, are to be answered in accordance with the following paragraphs.

41

Incentive zoning is an affirmative tool that has widespread applications. The Zoning Resolution which became effective in 1981 substantially reduced the amount of floor space that a developer could put up on a given size lot and increased the light and air. In the Chrysler Building, which was built under the old legislation, the floor space is 27 times the size of the lot. The maximum ratio allowed for buildings now without a special permit is 18.

The newer zoning ordinance provided incentives to developers to devote part of the plot to public plazas or arcades. This space is needed to supplement the sidewalks, which in many cases are as narrow as they were when the midtown area was lined with brownstone or brickfront houses.

While the newer zoning has produced plazas, it has not of itself proved to be a sufficient development control. Stretches of Third Avenue and the Avenue of the Americas, for example, have been almost completely redeveloped in the last few years. This massive private investment has produced several fine individual buildings. The total environment produced, however, has been disappointing in a number of respects, and there is nowhere near the amenity that there could have been.

4. According to the paragraphs above, the use of incentive zoning has not been entirely successful because it has

    A. discouraged redevelopment
    B. encouraged massive private development along Third Avenue
    C. been ineffective in controlling overall redevelopment
    D. not significantly increased the number of parks and plazas being built

5. According to the above paragraphs, one might conclude that before the new Zoning Resolution was passed,

    A. buildings on a given site were required to have greater setbacks
    B. the amount of private investment in development was significantly smaller than it is today
    C. no controls on development existed
    D. the provision of parks and plazas was less frequent

6. In the context of the above paragraphs, the word *amenity* means

    A. compliance with regulations
    B. correction of undesirable environmental aspects
    C. responsiveness to guidelines and incentives
    D. pleasant or desirable features

Questions 7-8.

DIRECTIONS: Questions 7 and 8 are to be answered in accordance with the following paragraphs.

We must also find better ways to handle the relocation of people uprooted by projects. In the past, many renewal plans have foundered on this problem, and it is still the most difficult part of community development. Large-scale replacement of low-income residents — many ineligible for public housing — has contributed to deterioration of surrounding communities, as in Manhattan's West Side, Coney Island, and Arverne. Recently, thanks to changes in Housing Authority procedures, relocation has been accomplished in a far more satisfactory fashion. The step-by-step community development projects we advocate in this plan should bring further improvement.

But additional measures will be necessary. There are going to be more people to be moved; and, with the current shortage of apartments, large ones especially, it is going to be tougher to find places to move them to. The city should have more freedom to buy or lease housing that comes on the market because of normal turnover and make it available to relocatees.

7. According to the above paragraphs, one of the reasons a neighborhood may deteriorate is that   7._____

   A. there is a scarcity of large apartments
   B. step-by-step community development projects have failed
   C. people in the given neighborhood are uprooted from their homes
   D. a nearby renewal project has an inadequate relocation plan

8. From the above paragraphs, one might conclude that the relocation phase of community renewal has been improved   8._____

   A. by changes in Housing Authority procedures
   B. by development of step-by-step community development projects
   C. through expanded city powers to buy housing for relocation
   D. through the Housing Authority Leasing Program

Questions 9-10.

DIRECTIONS: Questions 9 and 10 are to be answered in accordance with the following paragraphs.

Provision of decent housing for the lower half of the population (by income) was thus taken on as a public responsibility. Public housing was to assist the poorest quarter of urban families while the 221(d)(3) Housing Program would assist the next quarter. But limited funds meant that the supply of subsidized housing could not stretch nearly far enough to help this half of the population. Who were to be left out in the rationing process which was accomplished by the sifting of applicants for housing on the part of public and private authorities?

Discrimination on the grounds of race or color is not allowed under Federal law. In all sections of the country, encouragingly, housing programs are found which allow this law to the letter. Yet, housing programs in some cities still suffer from the residue of racial segregation policies and attitudes that for years were condoned or even encouraged.

Some sifting in the 221(d)(3) Housing Program follows the practice of many public housing authorities, the imposition of requirements with respect to character. This is a delicate matter. To fill a project overwhelmingly with broken families, alcoholics, criminals, delinquents, and other problem tenants would hardly make it a wholesome environment. Yet the total exclusion of such families is hardly an acceptable alternative. To the extent this exclusion is practiced, the very people whose lives are described in order to persuade lawmakers and the public to instigate new programs find the door shut in their faces when such programs come into being. The proper balance is difficult to achieve, but society's neediest families surely should not be totally denied the opportunities for rejuvenation in subsidized housing.

9. From the above paragraphs, it can be assumed that the 221(d)(3) Housing Program   9._____

   A. served a population earning more than the median income
   B. served a less affluent population than is served by public housing
   C. excludes all problem families from its projects
   D. is a subsidized housing program

10. According to the above paragraphs, the provision of housing for the poor   10._____

    A. has not been completely accomplished with public monies
    B. is never influenced by segregationist policies
    C. is limited to providing housing for only the neediest families
    D. is primarily the responsibility of the Federal government

Questions 11-12.

DIRECTIONS: Questions 11 and 12 are to be answered in accordance with the following paragraph.

Though the recent trend toward apartment construction may appear to be the region's response to large-lot zoning and centralized industry, it really is not. It is mainly a function of the age of the population (coupled with a rush to build apartments in the city between the passage of the newer zoning ordinance and its enforcement in December 1981). Most of the apartments are occupied by one- and two-person families — young people out of school but without a family of their own and older people whose children have grown. Both groups have been increasing in number; and, in this region, they characteristically live in apartments. It is this increased demand for apartments and the simultaneous decrease in demand for one-family houses that dramatically raised the percentage of building permits issued for multi-family housing units from 36 percent in 1977 to 67 percent in 1981. The fact that three-fourths of the apartments were built in the Core between 1977 and 1981 at the same time as the Core was losing population underscores the failure of the apartment boom to slow the outward spread of the population.

11. According to the above paragraph, one of the reasons for the increase in the number of building permits issued for multi-family construction in the city metropolitan region is   11._____

    A. that workers in industry want to live close to their jobs
    B. an increase in the number of elderly people living in the region
    C. the inability of many families to afford the large lots necessary to build private homes
    D. the new zoning ordinance made it easier to build apartments

12. According to the above paragraph, the apartment construction boom   12._____

    A. increased the population density in the core
    B. spurred a population shift to the suburbs
    C. did not halt the outward flow of the population from the core
    D. was most significant in the outer areas of the region

Questions 13-14.

DIRECTIONS: Questions 13 and 14 are to be answered in accordance with the following paragraphs.

The city's economy has its own dynamics, and there is only so much the government can do to shape it. But that margin is critically important. If the city uses its points of leverage, it can generate a large number of jobs and good jobs, jobs that lead to advancement.

As a major employer itself, the city can upgrade the jobs it offers and greatly improve its services to the public if it does so. Since highly skilled professionals will always be in short supply, the city must train more paraprofessionals to take over routine tasks. Equally important, it must provide them with a realistic job ladder so they can move on up — nurse's aide to certified nurse, for example, teacher's aide to teacher. The training programs for such upgrading will require a substantial public investment but the cost-benefit return should be excellent.

As a major purchaser of goods and services, the city can stimulate business enterprise in the ghetto. The growth of Black and Puerto Rican firms will produce more local jobs; it will also create the kind of managerial talent the ghetto needs.

New kinds of enterprise can be set up. In housing, for example, there is a huge backlog of rehabilitation work to be done and a large pool of unskilled manpower to be trained for it. Corporations can be formed to take over tenements, remodel, maintain, and operate them, as in the Brownsville Home Maintenance Program. Grocery cooperatives to bring food prices down are another possibility.

13. According to the above paragraphs, the city is the major employer and, by using its capacity, it can

    A. assist unskilled people with talent to move up on the job ladder
    B. create private enterprises that will renew all areas of the city in need of renewal
    C. eliminate poverty in the ghetto areas by selective purchase of goods and services
    D. have no influence on the economy of the city

14. According to the above paragraphs, one may REASONABLY conclude that

    A. the city has no power to influence the job market
    B. a by-product of strategic purchasing and employment and training practices can be the rehabilitation of housing and the lowering of food prices
    C. highly skilled professions, which are now in short supply, will no longer be needed after paraprofessionals are trained to take over routine jobs
    D. the city's major objective is to bring down food prices

15. 500 persons attended a public hearing at which a proposed public housing project was being considered. Less than half favored the project, while the majority opposed the project.
    According to the above statement, it is REASONABLE to conclude that

    A. the proposal stimulated considerable community interest
    B. the public housing project was disapproved by the city because a majority opposed it

C. those who opposed the project lacked sympathy for needy persons
D. the supporters of the project were led by militants

16. A document was published by a public agency and distributed for discussion. The document contained data showing trends in the level of reading among freshmen college students and suggested that the high schools were not investing enough effort in overcoming retardation. It compared the costs of intensifying reading instruction in the secondary schools as compared to costs in college for such instruction.
According to the above statement, it is REASONABLE to conclude that

A. the document proposed new programs
B. the college students read better than high school students
C. some college students need remedial reading
D. the study was done by a consultant

17. A vacant lot close to a polluted creek is for sale. Two buyers compete. One owns an adjacent factory which provides 300 high paying unskilled jobs. He needs to expand or move from the city. If he expands, he will provide 300 additional jobs. The other is a community group in a changing residential area close by. They hope to stabilize the neighborhood by bringing in new housing. They could build an apartment building with 100 dwelling units on the lot.
According to the above paragraph, it is REASONABLE to conclude that

A. jobs are more important than housing
B. there is conflict between the factory owners and the neighborhood group
C. the neighborhood group will not succeed in stabilizing the area by constructing new housing
D. the polluted creek should be cleaned up

Questions 18-21.

DIRECTIONS: Questions 18 through 21, inclusive, refer to the phrases shown below. For each of the questions, select that phrase which BEST completes the sentence for that question.

A. to increase training and educational opportunities
B. to remove social ills by a slum clearance program
C. to select the goals and values to which these resources should be directed
D. to diminish drastic redevelopment, to provide opportunities to move within the area, or to move to new areas which can be assimilated to old objectives

18. In addition to concern with the rational allocation of resources, the urban planning process needs _____.

19. The early housing reformers emphasized the inadequate physical environment of the slums, understressed the connection between the social environment of the slums and the disorders they wanted to cure, and attempted _____.

20. The objective for assisting the transition to middle class status will mean intensified efforts _____. 20.____

21. To provide a sense of continuity for those people whose residential areas are being renewed, mainly working class, it is desirable _____. 21.____

Questions 22-25.

DIRECTIONS: For Questions 22 through 25, select that item from Column B that is MOST closely related to the item in Column A.

COLUMN A	COLUMN B	
22. City Map	A. Citizen Participation	22.____
23. Revenue Sharing	B. Block Grants	23.____
24. Opportunity Structure	C. Streets	24.____
25. Public Hearing	D. Upward Mobility	25.____

KEY (CORRECT ANSWERS)

1.	B		11.	B
2.	D		12.	C
3.	C		13.	A
4.	C		14.	B
5.	D		15.	A
6.	D		16.	C
7.	D		17.	B
8.	A		18.	C
9.	D		19.	B
10.	A		20.	A

21. D
22. C
23. B
24. D
25. A

EXAMINATION SECTION
TEST 1

DIRECTIONS: Each question or incomplete statement is followed by several suggested answers or completions. Select the one that BEST answers the question or completes the statement. *PRINT THE LETTER OF THE CORRECT ANSWER IN THE SPACE AT THE RIGHT.*

Questions 1-5.

DIRECTIONS: Questions 1 through 5 are based on the table shown below.

POPULATION, URBAN AND RURAL, BY RACE: 2000 TO 2020

In thousands, except percent. An urbanized area comprises at least 1 city of 50,000 inhabitants (central city) plus contiguous, closely settled areas (urban fringe). Data for 2000 and 2010 according to urban definition used in the 2010 census; 2020 data according to the 2020 definition.

YEAR AND AREA	TOTAL	WHITE	ALL OTHER	PERCENT DISTRIBUTION		
				TOTAL	WHITE	ALL OTHER
2000, total population	151,326	135,150	16,176	100.0	100.0	100.0
Urban	96,847	86,864	9,983	64.0	64.3	61.7
Inside urbanized areas	69,249	61,925	7,324	45.8	45.8	45.3
Central cities	48,377	42,042	6,335	32.0	31.1	39.2
Urban fringe	20,872	19,883	989	13.8	14.7	6.1
Outside urbanized areas	27,598	24,939	2,659	18.2	18.5	16.4
Rural	54,479	48,286	6,193	36.0	35.7	38.3
2010, total population	179,323	158,832	20,491	100.0	100.0	100.0
Urban	125,269	110,428	14,840	69.9	69.5	72.4
Inside urbanized areas	95,848	83,770	12,079	53.5	52.7	58.9
Central cities	57,975	47,627	10,348	32.3	30.0	50.5
Urban fringe	37,873	36,143	1,371	21.1	22.8	8.4
Outside urbanized areas	29,420	26,658	2,762	16.4	16.8	13.5
Rural	54,054	48,403	5,651	30.1	30.5	27.6
2020, total population	203,212	177,749	25,463	100.0	100.0	100.0
Urban	149,325	128,773	20,552	73.5	72.4	80.7
Inside urbanized areas	118,447	100,952	17,495	58.3	56.8	68.7
Central cities	63,922	49,547	14,375	31.5	27.9	56.5
Urban fringe	54,525	51,405	3,120	26.8	28.9	12.3
Outside urbanized areas	30,878	27,822	3,057	15.2	15.7	12.0
Rural	53,887	48,976	4,911	26.5	27.6	19.3

1. The ratio of urban to rural population in 2000 was MOST NEARLY

   A. 3:1   B. 4:1   C. 2:1   D. 14:1

1.____

2. According to the table, the trend of population inside urban areas has been

   A. towards greater concentration   B. towards less concentration
   C. towards stabilization   D. erratic

2.____

3. Since 2000, the urban fringe white population has substantially increased while the urban fringe other population has

   A. slightly decreased
   B. greatly decreased
   C. remained the same
   D. increased moderately

4. Over the years, the percentage of the urban white population as compared with the percentage of the total urban population has

   A. remained relatively constant
   B. substantially decreased
   C. substantially increased
   D. varied

5. Select the one of the following which BEST describes the central city white population rate of decrease since 2000 as compared with the central city black population rate of increase.

   A. The central city white population rate of decrease has been greater than the central city black population rate of increase.
   B. The central city white and black populations have not increased to a significant degree.
   C. The central city white population rate of decrease has been equal to the central city black population rate of increase.
   D. The central city white population rate of decrease has been less than the central city black population rate of increase.

Questions 6-10.

DIRECTIONS: Questions 6 through 10 are to be answered on the basis of the table shown below.

STANDARDS FOR RECREATION AREAS

TYPE OF AREA	ACRES PER 1,000 POPULATION	SIZE OF SITE (ACRES) IDEAL	SIZE OF SITE (ACRES) MINIMUM	RADIUS OF AREA SERVED (MILES)
Playgrounds	1.5	4	2	0.5
Neighborhood parks	2.0	10	5	0.5
Playfields	1.5	15	10	1.5
Community parks	3.5	100	40	2.0
District parks	2.0	200	100	3.0
Regional parks and reservations	15.0	500-1,000	varies	10.0

6. What is the MINIMUM number of playfields that a community of 15,000 people may contain if the size of each is kept within the limits shown in the table?

   A. 4   B. 10   C. 6   D. 2

7. If, as far as possible, ideal sized playgrounds are built, how many IDEAL SIZED playgrounds should a community of 12,000 people contain?

   A. 4   B. 8   C. 1   D. 10

8. Approximately how many people can a community park of 200 acres serve? 8.____

   A. 120,000   B. 80,000   C. 55,000   D. 20,000

9. If only minimum sized neighborhood parks are built, how many will be required for a population of 20,000? 9.____

   A. 5   B. 2   C. 8   D. 12

10. A community of 75,000 persons is evenly distributed over a 5 square mile area. Of the following, the number and size of playgrounds that would BEST satisfy the standards is _____ playgrounds @ _____ acres each. 10.____

    A. 5; 7.5   B. 35; 3.5   C. 10; 10   D. 50; 1.5

11. The illustration shown at the right is an example of a 11.____

    A. simple grade separation
    B. simple interchange of a freeway with a highway
    C. three-level interchange
    D. T interchange

12. The practical MINIMUM number of cars per hour that can be carried per lane on a limited access roadway with uninterrupted flow is considered to be APPROXIMATELY 12.____

    A. 750   B. 1,500   C. 5,000   D. 10,000

13. A street that is open at only one end, with provision for a turn-around at the other, is called a 13.____

    A. local street   B. cul-de-sac
    C. loop street   D. minor street

14. Which of the following shopping center types is the local source of staple goods and daily services? 14.____

    A. Central Business District
    B. Regional Shopping Center
    C. Highway Strip Development
    D. Neighborhood Shopping Center

15. *Air rights* refers to the concept that 15.____

    A. all people are entitled to clean air
    B. vistas from apartments cannot be obstructed
    C. buildings can be constructed over railroads or highways
    D. buildings should be oriented towards the prevailing breezes

16. The one of the following LEAST likely to be considered an integral part of urban design is 16.____

    A. spatial forms   B. surfaces
    C. vistas   D. underground utilities

Questions 17-21.

DIRECTIONS: Questions 17 through 21 are based upon the table shown below.

LIVE BIRTHS, DEATHS, MARRIAGES, AND DIVORCES: 1940-1991

	Number (1,000)					Rate per 1,000 Population				
		DEATHS		MAR-	DIVOR-		DEATHS		MAR-	DIVOR-
YEAR	BIRTHS	TOTAL	INFANT	RIAGES	CES	BIRTHS	TOTAL	INFANT	RIAGES	CES
1940	2,777	697	(NA)	948	83	30.1	14.7	(NA)	10.3	0.9
1945	2,965	816	78	1,008	104	29.5	13.2	99.9	10.0	1.0
1950	2,950	1,118	130	1,274	171	27.7	13.0	85.8	12.0	1.6
1955	2,909	1,192	135	1,188	175	25.1	11.7	71.7	10.3	1.5
1960	2,618	1,327	142	1,127	196	21.3	11.3	64.6	9.2	1.6
1965	2,377	1,393	120	1,327	218	18.7	10.9	55.7	10.4	1.7
1970	2,559	1,417	111	1,596	264	19.4	10.8	47.0	12.1	2.0
1975	2,858	1,402	105	1,613	485	20.4	10.6	38.3	12.2	3.5
1980	3,632	1,452	104	1,667	385	24.1	9.6	29.2	11.1	2.6
1985	4,104	1,529	107	1,531	377	25.0	9.3	26.4	9.3	2.3
1990	4,258	1,712	111	1,523	393	23.7	9.5	26.0	8.5	2.2
1991	4,268	1,702	108	1,548	414	23.3	9.3	25.3	8.5	2.3

NA   Not Available

17. From 1940 to 1991, the birth rate has

    A. approximately doubled
    B. remained stable
    C. been reduced by 25%
    D. had two breaks in its downward progression

18. A comparison of the total population death rate to the infant death rate shows that

    A. the two rates have remained constant
    B. the infant death rate is greater
    C. the total population death rate has decreased at a faster rate
    D. infants had a greater chance to survive in 1965 than in 1980

19. In 1945, about one marriage out of 10 ended in divorce.
    In which of the following years would the rate be LESS?

    A. 1985   B. 1965   C. 1950   D. 1940

20. The significance of the decrease in the infant death rate is that

    A. family size will increase
    B. family size will decrease
    C. family size will not be affected
    D. children will become a smaller percentage of the total population

21. According to the chart, the total death rate declined from 14.7 in 1940 to 9.3 in 1991, yet each year more people have died. This fact is MOST likely accounted for by

    A. poor reporting techniques
    B. the decrease in the mortality rate
    C. the increase of total population
    D. the increase of older people in the total population

22. The type of interchange pictured in the illustration shown at the right is called a _____ interchange.

    A. simple
    B. cloverleaf
    C. universal
    D. Bel Geddes

23. This type of interchange (pictured in the preceding question) is used when

    A. topographic conditions are difficult
    B. traffic volumes are heavy
    C. a major and minor road intersect
    D. two major roads intersect

24. The one of the following basic requirements which would NOT be considered an integral part of a comprehensive plan is

    A. a capital improvement program
    B. physical design proposals
    C. long-range policy statements
    D. social and economic considerations

Questions 25-28.

DIRECTIONS: Questions 25 through 28 are based on the data shown below, which indicates total housing units.

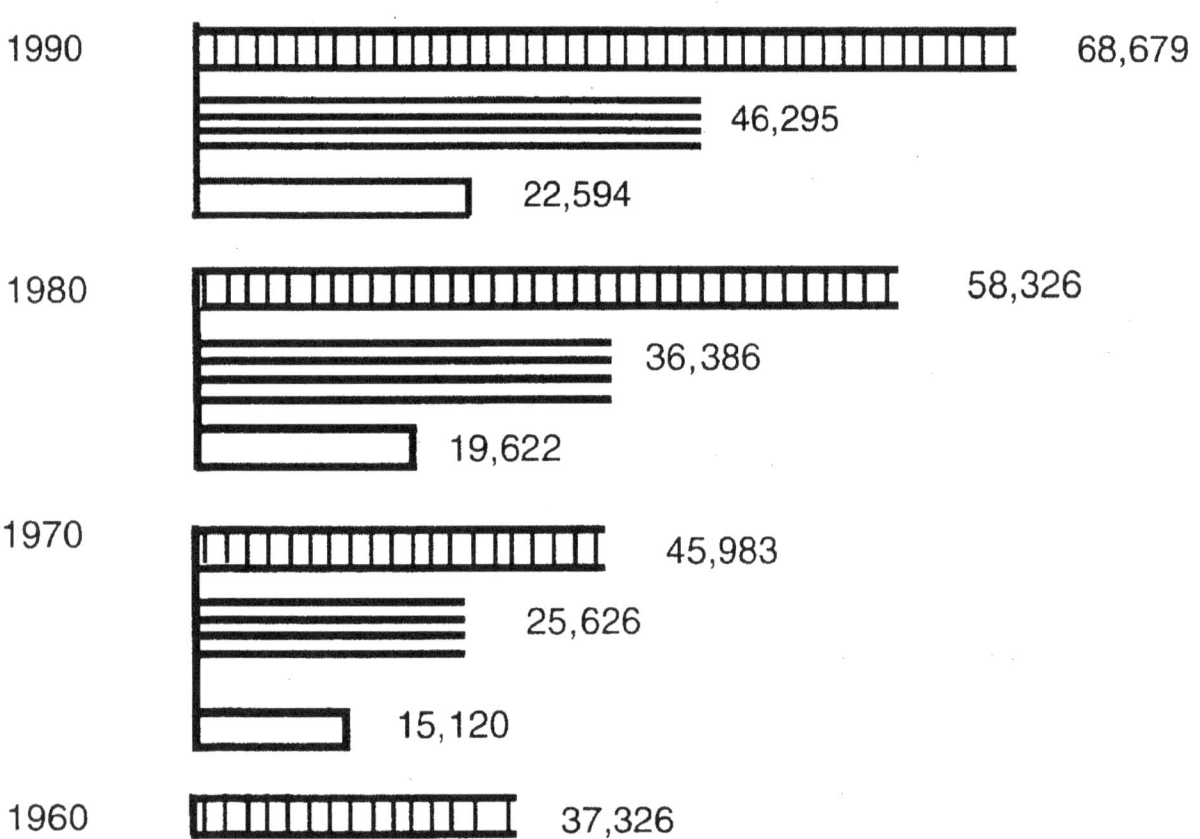

25. The period of GREATEST production of housing units was 25.____

    A. 1950-60   B. 1980-90   C. 1970-80   D. 1960-70

26. The location of the LARGEST gains in housing units since 1960 was in the 26.____

    A. suburban areas   B. central cities
    C. SMSA's   D. rural areas

27. Contrary to many misconceptions, the above data shows that the central cities are 27.____

    A. losing population to the suburbs
    B. keeping pace with the overall housing development
    C. showing strong development trends
    D. growing, but at a decreasing rate

28. Based on the above data, which of the following statements is MOST accurate? 28.____

    A. The housing stock is rapidly becoming outdated.
    B. More new homes are located in suburban areas than in central cities.
    C. The housing supply is rapidly catching up to the demand.
    D. The majority of the population is located in the SMSA's.

29. The name of the long-range schedule of major projects and their estimated costs over a period of 5-10 years is the 29.____

    A. budget
    B. comprehensive plan
    C. capital improvement program
    D. input-output program

30. *Cost Benefit Analysis* is a method used to 30.____

    A. determine budget compliance
    B. compare costs and benefits of a particular investment
    C. evaluate productivity in school construction
    D. establish social benefits for a neighborhood

31. A *workable program* is a SIGNIFICANT element of a(n) 31.____

    A. urban renewal program
    B. comprehensive plan
    C. capital improvement program
    D. urban design program

32. Which of the following would NOT be considered a major type of municipal planning agency in the United States? 32.____

    A. An independent planning commission
    B. The planning department
    C. A community development department
    D. A local renewal agency

33. Townhouses are MOST closely related to which of the following types of residential construction? 33.____

    A. Garden apartments   B. Row houses
    C. High-rise complexes   D. Semi-attached houses

34. The one of the following which could NOT be considered an accessory use in a residence district is a 34.____

    A. garage   B. greenhouse
    C. dwelling   D. storage shed

35. The ratio of parking space to retail floor area in a major regional shopping center would MOST often be 35.____

    A. 1:1   B. 3:1   C. 6:1   D. 10:1

KEY (CORRECT ANSWERS)

1.	C	16.	D
2.	A	17.	C
3.	D	18.	B
4.	A	19.	D
5.	D	20.	C
6.	D	21.	C
7.	A	22.	B
8.	C	23.	D
9.	C	24.	A
10.	B	25.	C
11.	A	26.	A
12.	B	27.	D
13.	B	28.	B
14.	D	29.	C
15.	C	30.	B

31. A
32. D
33. B
34. C
35. B

TEST 2

DIRECTIONS: Each question or incomplete statement is followed by several suggested answers or completions. Select the one that BEST answers the question or completes the statement. *PRINT THE LETTER OF THE CORRECT ANSWER IN THE SPACE AT THE RIGHT.*

1. When the term *density* is commonly employed as a measure of land use, it refers to the

    A. number of persons
    B. land coverage
    C. number of buildings
    D. number of dwelling units

2. The *City Beautiful* movement was an outgrowth of the

    A. Bauhaus School in 1920
    B. Chicago World's Fair in 1893
    C. N.Y.C. Zoning Ordinance of 1916
    D. planning concepts of Emilio Sitte

3. The American Greenbelt towns were built to

    A. create open space
    B. establish independent satellite communities
    C. establish residential *dormitory* communities
    D. disperse urban population

4. The FIRST United States Housing Act was passed by Congress in

    A. 1929   B. 1949   C. 1941   D. 1937

5. A specific ratio of permissible floor space to lot area is known as

    A. floor area ratio
    B. open space ratio
    C. sky exposure plane
    D. lot coverage

6. A *protective covenant* can BEST be described as a(n)

    A. zoning ordinance
    B. easement
    C. fire insurance policy
    D. deed restriction

7. Underground utility lines are PREFERRED by most planners rather than overhead lines because underground lines

    A. are more accessible for maintenance
    B. cost less
    C. are not visible
    D. are laid in proper easements

8. If a local street right-of-way is 50 feet, the paved width of the street is GENERALLY _____ feet.

    A. 18   B. 26   C. 44   D. 50

9. The term *zero population growth* refers to the concept that

   A. the population will eventually become extinct
   B. married couples will not bear children
   C. each family will produce only two children
   D. parents will be subject to a planned schedule of parenthood

10. The MOST common dimensions of a half-acre residential lot are

    A. 100 ft. x 100 ft.
    B. 100 ft. x 200 ft.
    C. 120 ft. x 150 ft.
    D. 200 ft. x 200 ft.

11. As a general rule, large street trees should be planted

    A. 25 feet apart
    B. 50-75 feet apart
    C. 150-200 feet apart
    D. spaced randomly

12. A key regulation of a zoning ordinance relates to the

    A. architectural style of a building
    B. slope of a site
    C. height and bulk of buildings
    D. subsoil conditions

13. Under which one of the following authorities are zoning ordinances adopted by local communities?

    A. Police power
    B. Community power
    C. Will of the people
    D. Common law

14. MOST state enabling laws require that zoning regulations be based upon a

    A. land use plan
    B. base map
    C. comprehensive plan
    D. topographical map

15. The OBJECTIVE of an *interim zoning ordinance* is to

    A. zone only a portion of the community for a special purpose
    B. maintain existing conditions until a more comprehensive ordinance is prepared
    C. create a special district
    D. allow greater freedom in interpretation and utilization of the zoning regulations

16. A *non-conforming* use is

    A. a use which requires special approval to remain
    B. a building that does not comply with yard or bulk regulations
    C. one that is not permitted in a specific district
    D. a building which is structurally unsafe

17. A variance is granted by a board of appeals to

    A. obtain financial relief
    B. provide a balance of power
    C. test community opinion
    D. relieve practical difficulty and hardship

18. Which of the following zoning regulations, taken by itself, would permit the MOST floor area of building on a specific lot?
    A

    A. floor area ratio of 3:1
    B. maximum lot coverage of 60%
    C. maximum building height of 50 feet
    D. parking ratio of 2:1

19. Sewers used to carry rain or surface water to a body of water so as to prevent flooding are called _____ sewers.

    A. sanitary   B. storm   C. combined   D. overflow

20. The *Garden City* concept was made famous through a book written by

    A. Sir Patrick Abercombie
    B. Patrick Geddes
    C. Ebenezer Howard
    D. Sir Raymond Unwin

21. *Broadacre City* was advocated as a concept of urban development by

    A. F.L. Wright
    B. Corbusier
    C. Saarinen
    D. Geddes

22. The man who can BEST be associated with the planning principle of *high density-low coverage* is

    A. Wright
    B. VanderRohe
    C. Saarinen
    D. Corbusier

23. The AVERAGE number of persons per household in the United States in 1970 was MOST NEARLY

    A. 2.0   B. 2.5   C. 3.0   D. 3.5

24. Which of the following methods would be the MOST accurate in making population projections?

    A. Migration and natural increase
    B. Apportionment
    C. School enrollment
    D. Geometric extrapolation

25. According to the 1990 census, the total population of the United States was MOST NEARLY _____ million persons.

    A. 190   B. 200   C. 280   D. 350

26. After the amounts of different land uses in a medium-size city have been tabulated, which of the following percentages of the total developed land would USUALLY be utilized for streets?

    A. 12%   B. 20%   C. 30%   D. 8%

27. During the past twenty years, the MOST significant factor causing reorientation of traditional urban land use patterns has been

   A. express highway construction
   B. airport development
   C. new schools
   D. permissive zoning ordinances

28. The fundamental objective of MOST suburban communities in attracting new industries is to

   A. increase local employment opportunities
   B. attract minority groups to relocate
   C. establish a balanced land use pattern
   D. increase tax income

29. Which of the following terms is NOT considered to be part of the street classification system?

   A. Major street
   B. Right-of-way
   C. Local street
   D. Cul-de-sac

30. The USUAL purpose for providing a water tower in a municipal water supply system is to

   A. establish a constant pressure
   B. increase the supply of water
   C. increase water pressure
   D. provide a reserve supply

31. The neighborhood unit concept, which includes the elementary school as its major element, was FIRST advocated in 1929 by

   A. Clarence Stein
   B. Henry Wright
   C. Clarence Perry
   D. N. Engelhardt

32. In the past few years, the type of housing which has received the LEAST amount of consideration in resolving the housing problem is

   A. cluster housing
   B. urban renewal
   C. public housing
   D. middle-income housing

33. *Performance standards* have become an INTEGRAL part of zoning ordinances relating to

   A. road construction
   B. industrial districts
   C. parking garages
   D. commercial areas

34. The legal concept upon which the exercise of *condemnation* is based is called the

   A. *due process* clause of the Constitution
   B. police power
   C. power of eminent domain
   D. general community welfare

35. In which of the following situations would the granting of a zoning variance be considered as IMPROPER action? A(n)

   A. serious topographic condition
   B. undersized lot held prior to zoning
   C. subsurface water condition
   D. economic loss due to a zone change

KEY (CORRECT ANSWERS)

1.	D		16.	C
2.	B		17.	D
3.	C		18.	B
4.	D		19.	B
5.	A		20.	C
6.	D		21.	A
7.	C		22.	D
8.	B		23.	B
9.	C		24.	A
10.	B		25.	C
11.	B		26.	C
12.	C		27.	A
13.	A		28.	D
14.	C		29.	B
15.	B		30.	A

31. C
32. C
33. B
34. C
35. D

TEST 3

DIRECTIONS: Each question or incomplete statement is followed by several suggested answers or completions. Select the one that BEST answers the question or completes the statement. *PRINT THE LETTER OF THE CORRECT ANSWER IN THE SPACE AT THE RIGHT.*

1. The MAJOR objective of cluster zoning is to provide

    A. greater densities
    B. a variety of housing types
    C. open space
    D. racial balance

    1._____

2. One tool in combating the problems of *spread city* is to provide

    A. improved mass transportation systems
    B. more major highways
    C. more single-family detached houses
    D. more community facilities

    2._____

3. The Environmental Protection Agency has issued national air quality standards for six common pollutants. The one of the following pollutants NOT included is

    A. sulfur oxides   B. carbon monoxide
    C. sulfur dioxide   D. hydrocarbon oxides

    3._____

4. The national air quality standards have been issued in two parts: primary and secondary standards. A PRIMARY standard is designed to

    A. protect public health
    B. protect public welfare
    C. establish ambient air quality
    D. prevent damage to the environment

    4._____

5. The MAJOR source of air pollution in many urban areas, according to the Environmental Protection Agency, is

    A. emissions from new plants
    B. fossil-fueled steam-generating plants
    C. motor vehicles
    D. large incinerators

    5._____

6. A technique designed for the analysis of national economies and which employs an industry interaction model appearing in the form of a multi-sector or industrial matrix is called

    A. economic base theory
    B. industrial complex analysis
    C. calculated forecasting
    D. input-output theory

    6._____

7. The traditional master plan, with its strong emphasis on physical improvements, is being more frequently replaced by

   A. policies planning
   B. normative planning
   C. quantitative analysis
   D. flexible planning

8. *Advocate planning* involves the planner in

   A. participating on a federal level to influence local officials
   B. working within the planning unit to obtain his desired goals
   C. working as a citizen, often as a protagonist against the local government
   D. preparing mathematical models of urban development

9. Of the following, the type of commercial development which is LEAST likely to be planned is a

   A. regional shopping center
   B. local shopping complex
   C. highway strip development
   D. central business district

10. The *official map* of a community designates all of the following EXCEPT

    A. street right-of-ways
    B. parks and playgrounds
    C. residential areas
    D. school sites

11. Land use intensity standards are MOST appropriately utilized with the development of

    A. standard subdivisions
    B. planned unit developments
    C. mobile home parks
    D. high-rise residential complexes

12. A topographic map does NOT generally express

    A. climatic conditions
    B. easements
    C. boundary lines and distances
    D. existing buildings

13. Clarence Stein contributed GREATLY to the development of

    A. the concept of the balanced community
    B. the design of Reston
    C. high-rise residential complexes
    D. the Radburn Plan

14. In site development, a 10% grade is considered MAXIMUM for

    A. streets and roads
    B. play fields
    C. building sites
    D. parking lots

15. The Model Cities Program includes all of the following EXCEPT

    A. job training in construction work
    B. local control of programs
    C. physical and social rehabilitation of a community
    D. new city design and development

16. HUD's *Operation Breakthrough* program encouraged

    A. fireproof buildings
    B. innovative prefabricated systems of construction
    C. speed of building erection
    D. a socio-economic assault on the housing program

17. A condominium can BEST be described as a

    A. high-rise residential complex with a complete range of amenities
    B. variation of cooperative ownership
    C. planned unit development with open space
    D. building with full ownership of the dwelling unit and common ownership of public areas

18. A MAJOR advantage of a leaching cesspool is that it

    A. can be used where ground water is two feet below grade
    B. can be used close to potable water
    C. requires a minimum of land area
    D. is limited in capacity

19. Land which rises 2 feet vertically to 5 feet horizontally has a slope of

    A. 2.5%   B. 20%   C. 25%   D. 40%

20. The MAJOR advantage of a subsoil disposal bed for sewage disposal is that it

    A. may be used in any soil except that rated as impervious
    B. is more economical to build
    C. requires less land area than that of a treatment plant
    D. may have a ground water level less than 2 feet below grade

21. To achieve the GREATEST amount of open space in the siting of houses, the one of the following patterns that a planner would MOST probably choose is a _____ pattern.

    A. gridiron   B. court
    C. cluster   D. free-form

22. The maximum distance a child should be required to walk to an elementary school is GENERALLY considered to be _____ mile.

    A. 1/4   B. 1/2   C. 3/4   D. 1

23. Modern industrial parks most often will include all of the following amenities EXCEPT

   A. landscaping and screening
   B. employee parking areas
   C. utilities and services
   D. multi-story structures

24. The BEST source of aerial photographs that provide the greatest coverage of the United States by a single agency is the

   A. Soil Conservation Service
   B. U.S. National Ocean Survey
   C. National Park Service
   D. Agricultural Stabilization Conservation Service

25. Terrain analysis is MOST closely related to the study of

   A. landforms   B. drainage
   C. soil   D. land erosion

26. Riparian rights deal with property that is located

   A. over mineral resources   B. along a body of water
   C. over railroad tracks   D. over a right-of-way

27. The ADVANTAGE of a *stol* port is that it

   A. can be located near another airport
   B. is not government regulated
   C. accommodates business and pleasure aircraft
   D. requires a short runway

28. One square mile contains EXACTLY _____ acres.

   A. 316   B. 444   C. 640   D. 1,000

29. The one of the following methods of refuse disposal that causes the LEAST air pollution, if efficiently carried out, is

   A. open dumping   B. land fill
   C. incineration   D. compositing

30. Sewers which collect sewage only from the plumbing systems of buildings and carry it to a sewage treatment plant are called _____ sewers.

   A. sanitary   B. storm
   C. combined   D. constant-flow

KEY (CORRECT ANSWERS)

1.	C	16.	B
2.	A	17.	D
3.	C	18.	C
4.	A	19.	D
5.	C	20.	A
6.	D	21.	C
7.	A	22.	B
8.	C	23.	D
9.	C	24.	D
10.	C	25.	A
11.	B	26.	B
12.	A	27.	D
13.	D	28.	C
14.	A	29.	B
15.	D	30.	A

EXAMINATION SECTION
TEST 1

DIRECTIONS: Each question consists of a statement. You are to indicate whether the statement is TRUE (T) or FALSE (F). *PRINT THE LETTER OF THE CORRECT ANSWER IN THE SPACE AT THE RIGHT.*

1. A building erected for rental purposes on a site is an over-improvement, when a less expensive building would result in a larger rate of return on the equity investment.   1.____

2. A "capital project" is any physical betterment or improvement or any preliminary studies or surveys relative thereto.   2.____

3. In planning a civic center, provision should be made (among others) for sites for municipal offices, high school, police and fire headquarters, public market, etc., if existing structures housing these activities need to be replaced.   3.____

4. Neighborhood parks, under accepted recreation standards, should have a minimum area of 1 acre per 1500 population to be served.   4.____

5. As a general principle, playfields are better located in large parks than as a part of high school sites.   5.____

6. Playgrounds for the 6-14 age group need to be spaced closer together than grade school sites.   6.____

7. The provision of intra-block playlots for pre-school age children is an accepted feature of modern subdivision layout.   7.____

8. A densely populated city which has 10 per cent of its total area in parks and playgrounds should be expected to be better provided with outdoor recreation space than an equivalent city with 15 acres of park per 1000 population, assuming equally good geographic distribution of the facilities in both cases.   8.____

9. In selecting a site for a suburban regional shopping center, it is *more important* to secure location adjacent to densely traveled highways than a location served by equivalent highways with a large reserve of traffic capacity.   9.____

10. As a step in estimating future public school enrollments, first grade enrollments of past years should be correlated with number of births six years prior, with quantitative allowance made for number of new dwelling units constructed in the intervening years.   10.____

11. In estimating future public school enrollments, it is good practice to make separate determinations of the number of children per family expected to enter school from: (a) new single family construction and (b) new multi-family dwelling construction.   11.____

12. As a means of relieving urban traffic congestion, the widening of city streets by acquisition of additional rights-of-way is generally *preferable* to construction of new arterial highways on new rights-of-way which require the same capital outlay for real estate.   12.____

13. Discharge capacity of a 60 m.p.h. express highway should be expected to be *greater* than discharge capacity of the same highway with a 40 m.p.h. enforced speed limit.   13.____

14. A progressive traffic light signal system, as compared with a simultaneous system, should be expected to *reduce* the driving speed of motor vehicles but to *increase* their average overall speed for distances in excess of two miles. 14.___

15. An express highway lane, reserved exclusively for modern buses, could carry 24,000 passengers per hour without standees. 15.___

16. The U.S. Department of Transportation may provide federal aid for state highway approaches to toll bridges. 16.___

17. Bypassing of through inter-city traffic will NOT solve street congestion in central business districts, in cities over 1,000,000 population. 17.___

18. In designing highway underpasses for mixed traffic, provision should be made for a vertical clearance of 15 feet. 18.___

19. Provision of public-aided housing projects for the aged is a feature of Dutch housing policy. 19.___

20. Anticipated need for future street widenings in new residential areas can be provided for by requiring building setbacks as a part of municipal subdivision regulations. 20.___

21. If a building has no setbacks or towers, the product of its percentage of lot coverage multiplied by its height in stories will give its "floor area ratio." 21.___

22. A special use (or special exception use), listed in a zoning ordinance as requiring special approval by the zoning board of appeals in a particular district, should ONLY be granted upon showing of proof of exceptional conditions and unnecessary hardship. 22.___

23. Courts have generally upheld a municipal zoning provision requiring a minimum floor area for a single-family house. 23.___

24. Under MOST zoning resolution provisions, site plans for large residential developments (75,000 sq. ft. of site and over) are subject to approval by both city planning commissions and Boards of Standards and Appeals. 24.___

25. A master plan program should be concerned with remote, future rather than current pressing problems. 25.___

26. Master plan studies should NOT be used until the whole plan is complete. 26.___

27. The public should NOT be informed of work being done on the master plan until it is ready for adoption. 27.___

28. Several base maps are required in planning, the scales of which vary with amount of detail a study involves. 28.___

29. A base map should ALWAYS show street names of all streets. 29.___

30. Large open spaces such as parks and cemeteries should *generally* be included on base maps to serve as land marks. 30.___

31. On maps to be reproduced at reduced size, lettering should be large enough to be readable when reduced. 31.___

32. It is NOT important to date a map relating to long-term plans. 32._____

33. The smaller the community, the more accurately population estimates can be made. 33._____

34. Surveys of pre-school age children affords accurate forecasts of public school enrollment. 34._____

35. The center of population is the geographic center of the developed area of a city. 35._____

KEY(CORRECT ANSWER)

1.	T	16.	T
2.	F	17.	T
3.	F	18.	F
4.	F	19.	T
5.	F	20.	T
6.	T	21.	T
7.	F	22.	F
8.	F	23.	T
9.	F	24.	T
10.	T	25.	F
11.	T	26.	F
12.	F	27.	F
13.	F	28.	T
14.	T	29.	F
15.	T	30.	T

31. T
32. F
33. F
34. F
35. F

TEST 2

DIRECTIONS: Each question consists of a statement. You are to indicate whether the statement is TRUE (T) or FALSE (F). *PRINT THE LETTER OF THE CORRECT ANSWER IN THE SPACE AT THE RIGHT.*

1. Bus transportation is *less* efficient than railroads in serving large masses of commuters. 1.____

2. Airports should be located at LEAST 20 miles beyond the developed area of a city. 2.____

3. "El" lines tend to *depreciate* values of property adjacent to them. 3.____

4. Traffic congestion can *usually* be eliminated by parking meters along the curb in central business districts. 4.____

5. A progressive traffic light system can be more readily installed where the blocks are short. 5.____

6. Sample manual counts to supplement automatic counters are *necessary* to determine truck flow. 6.____

7. The cordon count is a series of counts at various points along a highway. 7.____

8. Average day count is sufficient to determine points or area of congestion. 8.____

9. The largest portion of developed area of a self-contained city is used commercially, i.e.: for business and industry. 9.____

10. Land of *highest* value is usually occupied by industry. 10.____

11. Large cemeteries usually have an *adverse* effect on land values and highway transportation. 11.____

12. Strict control of smoke in industrial plants would *eliminate* the necessity for considering prevailing wind direction. 12.____

13. Zoning as now in effect will automatically eliminate the types of existing uses that do NOT belong in a district. 13.____

14. Limitation of building bulk by zoning is BEST attained by placing a maximum height restriction in the ordinance. 14.____

15. An unrestricted district is really an area NOT zoned. 15.____

16. Location of an express subway station has NO effect on land value pattern of a district. 16.____

17. Exclusion of dwellings in a heavy industrial zone is a *desirable* restriction. 17.____

18. All arterial highway borders should be zoned for business. 18.____

19. Increase in number of trucks makes railroad frontage no longer important in industrial location. 19.____

20. Elementary schools should be near centers of neighborhood units. 20.____

21. Diversification of industry is *advisable* particularly in small cities. 21._____

22. Economy in provision of water and sewer mains should result from properly administered zoning. 22._____

23. Building on undeveloped area *increases* storm water runoff. 23._____

24. Cost of installing and maintaining underground conduits for electricity is about the same as for overhead wire and poles. 24._____

25. Overhead electrical and telephone wires are less costly to install and maintain on curved streets than on a rectangular grid. 25._____

26. Sewer and water lines should be installed *before* streets are paved. 26._____

27. Areas should NOT be zoned for multiple family use until sewers are available. 27._____

28. A land value map is for the checking of fairness of assessments. 28._____

29. Character of land and accessibility are 2 *major* factors determining land values of undeveloped land. 29._____

30. A special assessment is added tax due to construction of a building on a lot. 30._____

31. Street trees are *more* appropriate in residential rather than business districts. 31._____

32. Offstreet parking is a *reasonable* zoning requirement for new business structures in outlying areas. 32._____

33. A basic industry of a city manufactures products sold outside the city. 33._____

34. Industrially used property, in general, produces tax revenue to the city in excess of cost of municipal services to such property. 34._____

35. All industry should be encouraged to remain or locate in the central district of a city. 35._____

KEY (CORRECT ANSWERS)

1.	T	16.	F
2.	F	17.	T
3.	T	18.	F
4.	F	19.	F
5.	F	20.	T
6.	T	21.	T
7.	F	22.	T
8.	F	23.	T
9.	F	24.	F
10.	F	25.	F
11.	T	26.	T
12.	F	27.	T
13.	F	28.	F
14.	F	29.	T
15.	F	30.	F

31. T
32. T
33. T
34. T
35. F

———

EXAMINATION SECTION
TEST 1

DIRECTIONS: Each question consists of a statement. You are to indicate whether the statement is TRUE (T) or FALSE (F). *PRINT THE LETTER OF THE CORRECT ANSWER IN THE SPACE AT THE RIGHT.*

1. A building erected for rental purposes on a site is an over-improvement, when a less expensive building would result in a larger rate of return on the equity investment. 1.____

2. A "capital project" is any physical betterment or improvement or any preliminary studies or surveys relative thereto. 2.____

3. In planning a civic center, provision should be made (among others) for sites for municipal offices, high school, police and fire headquarters, public market, etc., if existing structures housing these activities need to be replaced. 3.____

4. Neighborhood parks, under accepted recreation standards, should have a minimum area of 1 acre per 1500 population to be served. 4.____

5. As a general principle, playfields are better located in large parks than as a part of high school sites. 5.____

6. Playgrounds for the 6-14 age group need to be spaced closer together than grade school sites. 6.____

7. The provision of intra-block playlots for pre-school age children is an accepted feature of modern subdivision layout. 7.____

8. A densely populated city which has 10 per cent of its total area in parks and playgrounds should be expected to be better provided with outdoor recreation space than an equivalent city with 15 acres of park per 1000 population, assuming equally good geographic distribution of the facilities in both cases. 8.____

9. In selecting a site for a suburban regional shopping center, it is *more important* to secure location adjacent to densely traveled highways than a location served by equivalent highways with a large reserve of traffic capacity. 9.____

10. As a step in estimating future public school enrollments, first grade enrollments of past years should be correlated with number of births six years prior, with quantitative allowance made for number of new dwelling units constructed in the intervening years. 10.____

11. In estimating future public school enrollments, it is good practice to make separate determinations of the number of children per family expected to enter school from: (a) new single family construction and (b) new multi-family dwelling construction. 11.____

12. As a means of relieving urban traffic congestion, the widening of city streets by acquisition of additional rights-of-way is generally *preferable* to construction of new arterial highways on new rights-of-way which require the same capital outlay for real estate. 12.____

13. Discharge capacity of a 60 m.p.h. express highway should be expected to be *greater* than discharge capacity of the same highway with a 40 m.p.h. enforced speed limit. 13.____

14. A progressive traffic light signal system, as compared with a simultaneous system, should be expected to *reduce* the driving speed of motor vehicles but to *increase* their average overall speed for distances in excess of two miles. 14.____

15. An express highway lane, reserved exclusively for modern buses, could carry 24,000 passengers per hour without standees. 15.____

16. The U.S. Department of Transportation may provide federal aid for state highway approaches to toll bridges. 16.____

17. Bypassing of through inter-city traffic will NOT solve street congestion in central business districts, in cities over 1,000,000 population. 17.____

18. In designing highway underpasses for mixed traffic, provision should be made for a vertical clearance of 15 feet. 18.____

19. Provision of public-aided housing projects for the aged is a feature of Dutch housing policy. 19.____

20. Anticipated need for future street widenings in new residential areas can be provided for by requiring building setbacks as a part of municipal subdivision regulations. 20.____

21. If a building has no setbacks or towers, the product of its percentage of lot coverage multiplied by its height in stories will give its "floor area ratio." 21.____

22. A special use (or special exception use), listed in a zoning ordinance as requiring special approval by the zoning board of appeals in a particular district, should ONLY be granted upon showing of proof of exceptional conditions and unnecessary hardship. 22.____

23. Courts have generally upheld a municipal zoning provision requiring a minimum floor area for a single-family house. 23.____

24. Under MOST zoning resolution provisions, site plans for large residential developments (75,000 sq. ft. of site and over) are subject to approval by both city planning commissions and Boards of Standards and Appeals. 24.____

25. A master plan program should be concerned with remote, future rather than current pressing problems. 25.____

26. Master plan studies should NOT be used until the whole plan is complete. 26.____

27. The public should NOT be informed of work being done on the master plan until it is ready for adoption. 27.____

28. Several base maps are required in planning, the scales of which vary with amount of detail a study involves. 28.____

29. A base map should ALWAYS show street names of all streets. 29.____

30. Large open spaces such as parks and cemeteries should *generally* be included on base maps to serve as land marks. 30.____

31. On maps to be reproduced at reduced size, lettering should be large enough to be readable when reduced. 31.____

32. It is NOT important to date a map relating to long-term plans. 32.____

33. The smaller the community, the more accurately population estimates can be made. 33.____

34. Surveys of pre-school age children affords accurate forecasts of public school enrollment. 34.____

35. The center of population is the geographic center of the developed area of a city. 35.____

KEY(CORRECT ANSWER)

1.	T	16.	T
2.	F	17.	T
3.	F	18.	F
4.	F	19.	T
5.	F	20.	T
6.	T	21.	T
7.	F	22.	F
8.	F	23.	T
9.	F	24.	T
10.	T	25.	F
11.	T	26.	F
12.	F	27.	F
13.	F	28.	T
14.	T	29.	F
15.	T	30.	T

31.	T
32.	F
33.	F
34.	F
35.	F

TEST 2

DIRECTIONS: Each question consists of a statement. You are to indicate whether the statement is TRUE (T) or FALSE (F). *PRINT THE LETTER OF THE CORRECT ANSWER IN THE SPACE AT THE RIGHT.*

1. Bus transportation is *less* efficient than railroads in serving large masses of commuters. 1.____

2. Airports should be located at LEAST 20 miles beyond the developed area of a city. 2.____

3. "El" lines tend to *depreciate* values of property adjacent to them. 3.____

4. Traffic congestion can *usually* be eliminated by parking meters along the curb in central business districts. 4.____

5. A progressive traffic light system can be more readily installed where the blocks are short. 5.____

6. Sample manual counts to supplement automatic counters are *necessary* to determine truck flow. 6.____

7. The cordon count is a series of counts at various points along a highway. 7.____

8. Average day count is sufficient to determine points or area of congestion. 8.____

9. The largest portion of developed area of a self-contained city is used commercially, i.e.: for business and industry. 9.____

10. Land of *highest* value is usually occupied by industry. 10.____

11. Large cemeteries usually have an *adverse* effect on land values and highway transportation. 11.____

12. Strict control of smoke in industrial plants would *eliminate* the necessity for considering prevailing wind direction. 12.____

13. Zoning as now in effect will automatically eliminate the types of existing uses that do NOT belong in a district. 13.____

14. Limitation of building bulk by zoning is BEST attained by placing a maximum height restriction in the ordinance. 14.____

15. An unrestricted district is really an area NOT zoned. 15.____

16. Location of an express subway station has NO effect on land value pattern of a district. 16.____

17. Exclusion of dwellings in a heavy industrial zone is a *desirable* restriction. 17.____

18. All arterial highway borders should be zoned for business. 18.____

19. Increase in number of trucks makes railroad frontage no longer important in industrial location. 19.____

20. Elementary schools should be near centers of neighborhood units. 20.____

21. Diversification of industry is *advisable* particularly in small cities. 21.____

22. Economy in provision of water and sewer mains should result from properly administered zoning. 22.____

23. Building on undeveloped area *increases* storm water runoff. 23.____

24. Cost of installing and maintaining underground conduits for electricity is about the same as for overhead wire and poles. 24.____

25. Overhead electrical and telephone wires are less costly to install and maintain on curved streets than on a rectangular grid. 25.____

26. Sewer and water lines should be installed *before* streets are paved. 26.____

27. Areas should NOT be zoned for multiple family use until sewers are available. 27.____

28. A land value map is for the checking of fairness of assessments. 28.____

29. Character of land and accessibility are 2 *major* factors determining land values of undeveloped land. 29.____

30. A special assessment is added tax due to construction of a building on a lot. 30.____

31. Street trees are *more* appropriate in residential rather than business districts. 31.____

32. Offstreet parking is a *reasonable* zoning requirement for new business structures in outlying areas. 32.____

33. A basic industry of a city manufactures products sold outside the city. 33.____

34. Industrially used property, in general, produces tax revenue to the city in excess of cost of municipal services to such property. 34.____

35. All industry should be encouraged to remain or locate in the central district of a city. 35.____

3 (#2)

KEY (CORRECT ANSWERS)

1.	T	16.	F
2.	F	17.	T
3.	T	18.	F
4.	F	19.	F
5.	F	20.	T
6.	T	21.	T
7.	F	22.	T
8.	F	23.	T
9.	F	24.	F
10.	F	25.	F
11.	T	26.	T
12.	F	27.	T
13.	F	28.	F
14.	F	29.	T
15.	F	30.	F

31. T
32. T
33. T
34. T
35. F

EXAMINATION SECTION
TEST 1

DIRECTIONS: Each question consists of a statement. You are to indicate whether the statement is TRUE (T) or FALSE (F). *PRINT THE LETTER OF THE CORRECT ANSWER IN THE SPACE AT THE RIGHT.*

1. In 1916, New York City adopted the first comprehensive zoning ordinance in this country.   1.____

2. Since that time, American cities, with numerous exceptions, have adopted zoning ordinances so that now over 1,100 cities with populations in excess of 10,000 are zoned.   2.____

3. It is purely academic for the broker or salesman to be knowledgeable of planning, zoning, restrictive covenants, and other land use controls.   3.____

4. The purchaser, when he signs the usual form of purchase contract, agrees to take the land subject to restrictions of record, zoning, and other ordinances.   4.____

5. To the purchaser, use limitations are NOT usually so important as technical flaws on title that may be uncovered by examination of the abstract of title.   5.____

6. False information, intentionally or negligently given about land use restrictions, may be grounds for setting the sale aside.   6.____

7. Covenants that *run with the land* may be binding on those who inherit, buy or otherwise acquire the land after the owner of the land.   7.____

8. Restrictions imposed by subdivision developers are few in number and uniform in purpose.   8.____

9. Great care should be taken NOT to burden the land unduly because once on the land, they are hard to eliminate.   9.____

10. Many people, when the phrase *restrictive covenant* is used, think ONLY of racial or religious restrictions on land use.   10.____

11. Easements are SELDOM used by developers to implement their private plans.   11.____

12. *Conservation easements,* like privately imposed easements, will become increasingly important encumbrances on more and more tracts of land.   12.____

13. An existing filling station in a district zoned residential is an example of a non-conforming use.   13.____

14. For practical political reasons and in order to protect the zoning from attack on constitutional grounds, zoning ordinances uniformly permit the continuance of non-conforming uses.   14.____

15. An illegal use is one established before enactment of a zoning ordinance and in violation of it.   15.____

16. A method of bringing zoning into line with the prospective buyer's wishes is through the so-called zoning *variance*.   16.____

17. The zoning exception or special use permit is a method to meet the objectives of a prospective seller in appropriate cases. 17._____

18. It is a fact that the subdivider lays down an indelible land use pattern which will enhance or blight the community for generations to come. 18._____

19. The object of the official map is to preserve the land needed for future streets or for street-widening at bare land prices. 19._____

20. The restrictive covenant is the PRINCIPAL legal tool for the accomplishment of private land use planning goals. 20._____

21. Because land is rural, it is NOT zoned. 21._____

22. Zoning deals PRINCIPALLY with so-called bulk and density controls. 22._____

23. Land use planning may be both private and public. 23._____

24. In the absence of legal restraints, landowners exercising their broad common-law privileges of use may so use their land as to defeat both private or public planners goals and expectations. 24._____

25. Where a landowner stopped a non-conforming use some time ago and is now offering his premises for sale, the right to resume the use may have been lost by abandonment. 25._____

KEY (CORRECT ANSWERS)

1.	T	11.	F
2.	F	12.	T
3.	F	13.	T
4.	T	14.	T
5.	F	15.	F
6.	T	16.	T
7.	T	17.	F
8.	F	18.	T
9.	T	19.	T
10.	T	20.	T

21.	F
22.	F
23.	T
24.	T
25.	T

TEST 2

DIRECTIONS: Each question consists of a statement. You are to indicate whether the statement is TRUE (T) or FALSE (F). *PRINT THE LETTER OF THE CORRECT ANSWER IN THE SPACE AT THE RIGHT.*

1. The real estate business in the United States is largely concerned with the land and buildings in highly concentrated areas of population which we call cities, metropolitan areas, or urban communities. 1.____

2. Zoning may retard value decline but it CANNOT prevent it. 2.____

3. There is little consistency in zoning symbols and descriptions in the political subdivisions of state government. 3.____

4. Government is involved in the real estate business at the federal level but NOT at the state and local levels. 4.____

5. The subdivision laws are designed primarily to protect the seller from misrepresentation, deceit, and fraud in the sale of new subdivisions by disclosing to the prospective purchaser the pertinent facts concerning the project. 5.____

6. Where one lot in a subdivision is made security for the payment of a trust, deed, note, or other lien or encumbrance to be satisfied with the payment of money, this is called a *blanket encumbrance*. 6.____

7. The power of eminent domain is the same as the *police power*. 7.____

8. The MAIN issue in almost all condemnation or eminent domain cases is the amount of *just compensation* required to be paid to the attorneys. 8.____

9. A defined channel is any natural watercourse even though dry during a good portion of the year. 9.____

10. If water is flowing in a defined channel, a landowner may obstruct or direct such water. 10.____

11. Waters overflowing a defined channel are considered *floodwaters,* and any landowner may protect himself from them by reasonable methods even though this might result in the floodwaters entering another man's land. 11.____

12. A purchaser of a condominium owns the air space in which his particular unit is situated in fee simple, has a deed thereto, gets a separate tax assessment, and may apply for and acquire a title insurance policy on his property. 12.____

13. Land development generally means the creation of a *subdivision.* 13.____

14. Before starting a land development program, the prudent developer will first contact the county surveyor. 14.____

15. *Subdivision* does NOT include certain types of multi-family structures. 15.____

16. A person may sell or offer for sale a lot or parcel of land in a subdivision pending final approval from the proper authorities. 16.____

81

17. The approval of the tentative map of the subdivision submitted to the planning commission constitutes a final approval of the plat for recording.   17._____

18. The survey and plat of the subdivision may be made by a surveyor who is NOT a registered engineer or a licensed land surveyor.   18._____

19. The plat of the subdivision must be of such a scale that survey and mathematical information and other details can be easily obtained from it.   19._____

20. Before a plat is approved, all taxes and assessments MUST be paid.   20._____

21. Before any sales can be made of subdivided lands, certain documents and instruments must be placed in escrow with a legal escrow depository.   21._____

22. The law prohibits any person selling or offering to sell lots or parcels in a subdivision from issuing, circulating, or publishing any prospectus.   22._____

23. The law prohibits any person selling or offering to sell lots or parcels in a subdivision from making any statement or representation UNLESS he declares that the real estate subdivision has been approved or indorsed by the commission.   23._____

24. The law prohibits any person selling or offering to sell lots or parcels in a subdivision from issuing, circulating, or publishing any advertising matter UNLESS he does so anonymously.   24._____

25. The real estate commission or commissioner is generally given authority to issue a *cease or desist* order whenever he finds a subdivider violating any provisions of the subdivision act.   25._____

KEY (CORRECT ANSWERS)

1.	T	11.	T
2.	T	12.	T
3.	T	13.	T
4.	F	14.	T
5.	F	15.	F
6.	F	16.	F
7.	F	17.	F
8.	F	18.	F
9.	T	19.	T
10.	F	20.	T

21. T
22. F
23. F
24. F
25. T

TEST 3

DIRECTIONS: Each question consists of a statement. You are to indicate whether the statement is TRUE (T) or FALSE (F). *PRINT THE LETTER OF THE CORRECT ANSWER IN THE SPACE AT THE RIGHT.*

1. The purchaser, when he signs the USUAL form of purchase contract, agrees to take the land exempt from restrictions of record, zoning, and other municipal ordinances. 1.____

2. False information, intentionally or negligently given about land use restrictions, MAY be grounds for setting the sale aside. 2.____

3. Standing silently by when you know the prospect is intending to use the land for a purpose forbidden by public or private restrictions will NOT endanger the sale unless the prospect is intentionally led astray. 3.____

4. It is important for the broker or salesman to know the ways in which zoning restrictions can be changed and whether or not a change in the zoning restrictions on a certain piece of property is possible to enhance the possibilities of a sale. 4.____

5. In the absence of legal restraints, land owners exercising their broad common law privileges of use may so use their land as to defeat both private or public planners' goals and expectations. 5.____

6. The easement is the PRINCIPAL legal tool for the accomplishment of private land use planning goals. 6.____

7. It is possible through covenants to set up virtually a private municipal government by creating a neighborhood association, giving it power to police the residential and other use restrictions, maintain streets, provide water, or render other services and assess charges against the benefited lots so as to raise the money needed to finance the services. 7.____

8. A covenant restriction is USUALLY of a very minor nature. 8.____

9. Covenants may NOT be recorded. 9.____

10. Once a covenant is in effect, it is binding and can NEVER be removed. 10.____

11. No state may act through its courts or otherwise to enforce racial or religious land use restrictive covenants. 11.____

12. Set-back, side yard, and back yard requirements are common restrictions imposed by covenants. 12.____

13. Presence of a covenant based on religion or race will bar Federal Housing Administration mortgage insurance and Veterans Administration financing. 13.____

14. Sometimes set-backs from the street take the form of easements established by declaration or grant. 14.____

15. Brokers and salesmen have an obligation to know about the existence of both publicly purchased and privately imposed easements as well as about restrictive covenants so that prospective buyers can be informed. 15.____

16. Zoning consists of dividing the land within a given governmental unit into districts and then specifying what uses are permitted and which ones prohibited in each district. 16._____

17. Zoning does NOT deal with the placement and height of buildings on the land and with bulk and density controls. 17._____

18. There are ONLY three types of zones: residential, commercial, and industrial. 18._____

19. In modern zoning plans, industry is barred from residential areas, but residences may be built in industrial areas. 19._____

20. It is safe to assume that rural land is unzoned. 20._____

21. A non-conforming use is one which was in existence when zoning went into effect and which is inconsistent with zoning purposes. 21._____

22. Zoning ordinances uniformly PROHIBIT the continuance of non-conforming uses in zoning ordinances. 22._____

23. There is USUALLY a prohibition against the expansion of non-conforming uses in zoning ordinances. 23._____

24. Once a non-conforming use has been abandoned, it can ALWAYS be re-established. 24._____

25. A landowner whose use is non-conforming may NOT sell his land and pass on the right to continue the use to the buyer. 25._____

KEY (CORRECT ANSWERS)

1.	F	11.	T
2.	T	12.	T
3.	F	13.	T
4.	T	14.	T
5.	T	15.	T
6.	F	16.	T
7.	T	17.	F
8.	F	18.	F
9.	F	19.	F
10.	F	20.	F

21. T
22. F
23. T
24. T
25. F

TEST 4

DIRECTIONS: Each question consists of a statement. You are to indicate whether the statement is TRUE (T) or FALSE (F). *PRINT THE LETTER OF THE CORRECT ANSWER IN THE SPACE AT THE RIGHT.*

1. Where a buyer is purchasing a non-conforming structure, the broker should warn him that in case of substantial destruction by fire or otherwise, zoning may bar rebuilding. 1._____

2. Where a landowner stopped the non-conforming use some time ago and now is offering his premises for sale, the right to resume the use may have been lost by abandonment. 2._____

3. There is no difference between a variance and a special use permit. 3._____

4. Wherever federal law is applicable, it is paramount. 4._____

5. Ordinarily, the basis of federal law is interstate commerce. 5._____

6. This is true of the U.S. Supreme Court case Jones v. Mayer and Title VIII of the Civil Rights Act of 1968. 6._____

7. Title VIII applies even to the MOST local transactions. 7._____

8. What discrimination state laws do NOT prohibit, federal law now does. 8._____

9. While no one may refuse to sell, lease, or rent to another because of race or color, a real estate licensee may do so when acting under his principal's directions. 9._____

10. Should a principal seek to restrict a listing according to race or color, the licensee MUST refuse to accept the listing. 10._____

11. Title VIII prohibits denial of membership or participation in a real estate board or multiple listing service to a person because of race, color, religion, or national origin, or discrimination against him in terms or conditions of membership. 11._____

12. Real estate licensees must not discriminate but they may accept restrictive listings. 12._____

Questions 13-22.

DIRECTIONS: In each of the following questions, a blank space indicates that a word or phrase has been omitted. Supply the missing word or phrase that will complete the statement correctly.

13. Before subdivided land can be sold or leased, a notice of _____ MUST be filed with the commissioner. 13._____

14. In MOST cases, the owner and subdivider are the same, but sometimes the owner will turn over the land to someone else to develop and assume necessary authority to offer it for sale. This person is commonly known as a _____. 14._____

15. The _____ type of subdivision is the kind MOST frequently developed. 15._____

16. A _____ is an estate in real property consisting of an undivided interest in common in a portion of a parcel of real property together with a separate interest in space in a residential, industrial, or commercial building on such real property, such as an apartment, office, or store, and may include, in addition, a separate interest in other portions of such property. 16.____

17. The power of eminent domain is _____ the *police power*. 17.____

18. The power of eminent domain involves a _____ and the payment of compensation to the property owner. 18.____

19. The use of the power of eminent domain is often referred to as _____. 19.____

20. The MAIN issue in almost all eminent domain cases is the amount of _____ required to be paid to the property owner. 20.____

21. _____ is a general principle underlying a vast body of detailed water law. 21.____

22. Waters overflowing a defined channel are considered _____. 22.____

Questions 23-25.

DIRECTIONS: In continuous discourse, briefly and concisely answer the following questions.

23. What is a stock cooperative? 23.____
24. What is meant by a blanket encumbrance. 24.____
25. What is meant by *fair market value*? 25.____

KEY (CORRECT ANSWERS)

1. T
2. T
3. F
4. T
5. T
6. F
7. T
8. T
9. F
10. T
11. T
12. F
13. intention
14. subdivider
15. standard
16. condominium

17. different from
18. taking
19. condemnation
20. just compensation
21. Conservation
22. floodwaters
23. A stock cooperative is a corporation which is formed or availed of primarily for the purpose of holding title to, either in fee simple or for a term of years, improved real property, if all or substantially all of the stockholders of such corporation receive a right of exclusive occupancy in a portion of the real property, title to which is held by the corporation, which right of occupancy is transferrable only concurrently with the transfer of the share or shares of stock in the corporation held by the person having such right of occupancy.
24. A blanket encumbrance is where more than one lot in a subdivision is made security for the payment of a trust deed note or other lien or encumbrance to be satisfied with the payment of money.
25. Fair market value is the highest price land would bring if exposed for sale in the open market with reasonable time allowed to find a purchaser with knowledge of all uses and purposes to which the land is adapted, the seller not being required to sell or the purchaser required to purchase.

READING COMPREHENSION
UNDERSTANDING AND INTERPRETING WRITTEN MATERIAL
EXAMINATION SECTION
TEST 1

DIRECTIONS: Each question or incomplete statement is followed by several suggested answers or completions. Select the one that BEST answers the question or completes the statement. *PRINT THE LETTER OF THE CORRECT ANSWER IN THE SPACE AT THE RIGHT.*

Questions 1-3.

DIRECTIONS: Questions 1 through 3 are to be answered SOLELY on the basis of the following paragraph.

The aging housing inventory presents a broad spectrum of conditions, from good upkeep to unbelievable deterioration. Buildings, even relatively good buildings, are likely to have numerous minor violations rather than the gross and evident sanitary violations of an earlier age. Except for the serious violations in a relatively small number of slum buildings, the task is to deal with masses of minor violations that, though insignificant in themselves, amount in the aggregate to major deprivations of health and comfort to tenants. Caused by wear and tear, by the abrasions of time, and aggravated by neglect, these conditions do not readily yield to the dramatic *vacate and restore* measures of earlier times. Moreover, the lines between *good* and *bad* housing have become blurred in many parts of our cities; we find a range of *shades of gray* blending into each other. Different kinds of code enforcement efforts may be required to deal with different degrees of deterioration.

1. The above passage suggests that code enforcement efforts may have to be

    A. developed to cope with varying levels of housing dilapidation
    B. aimed primarily at the serious violations in slum buildings
    C. modeled on the *vacate and restore* measures of earlier times
    D. modified to reduce unrealistic penalties for petty violations

2. According to the above passage, during former times some buildings had sanitary violations which were

    A. irreparable and minor
    B. blurred and gray
    C. flagrant and obvious
    D. insignificant and numerous

3. According to the above passage, the aging housing stock presents a

    A. great number of rent-controlled buildings
    B. serious problem of tenant-caused deterioration
    C. significant increase in buildings without intentional violations
    D. wide range of physical conditions

Questions 4-5.

DIRECTIONS: Questions 4 and 5 are to be answered SOLELY on the basis of the following passage.

In general, housing code provisions relating to the safe and sanitary maintenance of dwelling units prescribe the maintenance required for foundations, walls, ceilings, floors, windows, doors, stairways, and also the facilities and equipment required in other sections. The more recent codes have, in addition, extensive provisions designed to ensure that the unit be maintained in a rat-free and rat-proof condition. Also, as an example of new approaches in code provisions, one proposed Federal model housing code prohibits the landlord from terminating vital services and utilities except during temporary emergencies or when actual repairs or maintenance are in process. This provision may be used to prevent a landlord from turning off utility services as a technique of self-help eviction or as a weapon against rent strikes.

4. According to the above passage, the more recent housing codes have extensive provisions designed to

    A. maintain a reasonably fire-proof living unit
    B. prohibit tenants from participating in rent strikes
    C. maintain the unit free from rats
    D. prohibit tenants from using lead-based paints

5. According to the above passage, one housing code would permit landlords to terminate vital services during

    A. a rent strike
    B. an actual eviction
    C. a temporary emergency
    D. the planning of repairs and maintenance

Questions 6-8.

DIRECTIONS: Questions 6 through 8 are to be answered SOLELY on the basis of the following passage.

City governments have long had building codes which set minimum standards for building and for human occupancy. The code (or series of codes) makes provisions for standards of lighting and ventilation, sanitation, fire prevention, and protection. As a result of demands from manufacturers, builders, real estate people, tenement owners, and building-trades unions, these codes often have established minimum standards well below those that the contemporary society would accept as a rock-bottom minimum. Codes often become outdated so that meager standards in one era become seriously inadequate a few decades later as society"s concept of a minimum standard of living changes. Out-of-date codes, when still in use, have sometimes prevented the introduction of new devices and modern building techniques. Thus, it is extremely important that building codes keep pace with changes in the accepted concept of a minimum standard of living.

6. According to the above passage, all of the following considerations in building planning would probably be covered in a building code EXCEPT

   A. closet space as a percentage of total floor area
   B. size and number of windows required for rooms of differing sizes
   C. placement of fire escapes in each line of apartments
   D. type of garbage disposal units to be installed

7. According to the above passage, if an ideal building code were to be created, how would the established minimum standards in it compare to the ones that are presently set by city governments?
   They would

   A. be lower than they are at present
   B. be higher than they are at present
   C. be comparable to the present minimum standards
   D. vary according to the economic group that sets them

8. On the basis of the above passage, what is the reason for difficulties in introducing new building techniques?

   A. Builders prefer techniques which represent the rock-bottom minimum desired by society.
   B. Certain manufacturers have obtained patents on various building methods to the exclusion of new techniques.
   C. The government does not want to invest money in techniques that will soon be outdated.
   D. New techniques are not provided for in building codes which are not up-to-date.

Questions 9-11.

DIRECTIONS: Questions 9 through 11 are to be answered SOLELY on the basis of the following paragraph.

When constructed within a multiple dwelling, such storage space shall be equipped with a sprinkler system and also with a system of mechanical ventilation in no way connected with any other ventilating system. Such storage space shall have no opening into any other part of the dwelling except through a fireproof vestibule. Any such vestibule shall have a minimum superficial floor area of fifty square feet, and its maximum area shall not exceed seventy-five square feet. It shall be enclosed with incombustible partitions having a fire-resistive rating of three hours. The floor and ceiling of such vestibule shall also be of incombustible material having a fire-resistive rating of at least three hours. There shall be two doors to provide access from the dwelling, to the car storage space. Each such door shall have a fire-resistive rating of one and one-half hours and shall be provided with a device to prevent the opening of one door until the other door is entirely closed.

9. According to the above paragraph, the one of the following that is REQUIRED in order for cars to be permitted to be stored in a multiple dwelling is a(n)

   A. fireproof vestibule   B. elevator from the garage
   C. approved heating system   D. sprinkler system

10. According to the above paragraph, the one of the following materials that would NOT be acceptable for the walls of a vestibule connecting a garage to the dwelling portion of a building is

    A. 3" solid gypsum blocks
    B. 4" brick
    C. 4" hollow gypsum blocks, plastered both sides
    D. 6" solid cinder concrete blocks

10._____

11. According to the above paragraph, the one of the following that would be ACCEPTABLE for the width and length of a vestibule connecting a garage that is within a multiple dwelling to the dwelling portion of the building is

    A. 3'8" x 13'0"   B. 4'6" x 18'6"
    C. 4'9" x 14'6"   D. 4'3" x 19'3"

11._____

Questions 12-13.

DIRECTIONS: Questions 12 and 13 are to be answered SOLELY on the basis of the following paragraph.

It shall be unlawful to place, use, or maintain in a condition intended, arranged, or designed for use, any gas-fired cooking appliance, laundry stove, heating stove, range or water heater or combination of such appliances in any room or space used for living or sleeping in any new or existing multiple dwelling unless such room or space has a window opening to the outer air or such gas appliance is vented to the outer air. All automatically operated gas appliances shall be equipped with a device which shall shut off automatically the gas supply to the main burners when the pilot light in such appliance is extinguished. A gas range or the cooking portion of a gas appliance incorporating a room heater shall not be deemed an automatically operated gas appliance. However, burners in gas ovens and broilers which can be turned on and off or ignited by non-manual means shall be equipped with a device which shall shut off automatically the gas supply to those burners when the operation of such non-manual means fails.

12. According to the above paragraph, an automatic shut-off device is NOT required on a gas

    A. hot water heater   B. laundry dryer
    C. space heater   D. range

12._____

13. According to the above paragraph, a gas-fired water heater is permitted

    A. only in kitchens   B. only in bathrooms
    C. only in living rooms   D. in any type of room

13._____

Questions 14-18.

DIRECTIONS: Questions 14 through 18 are to be answered SOLELY on the basis of the information contained in the statement below.

No multiple dwelling shall be erected to a height in excess of one and one-half times the width of the widest street on which it faces, except that above the level of such height, for each one foot that the front wall of such dwelling sets back from the street line, three feet shall be added to the height limit of such dwelling, but such dwelling shall not exceed in maximum height three feet plus one and three-quarter times the width of the widest street on which it faces.

Any such dwelling facing a street more than one hundred feet in width shall be subject to the same height limitations as though such dwelling faced a street one hundred feet in width.

14. The MAXIMUM height of a multiple dwelling set back five feet from the street line and facing a 60 foot wide street is _____ feet.   14.____

    A. 60   B. 90   C. 105   D. 165

15. The MAXIMUM height of a multiple dwelling set back six feet from the street line and facing a 120 foot wide street is _____ feet.   15.____

    A. 198   B. 168   C. 120   D. 105

16. The MAXIMUM height of a multiple dwelling is   16.____

    A. 100 ft.   B. 150 ft.   C. 178 ft.   D. unlimited

17. The MAXIMUM height of a multiple dwelling set back 10 feet from the street line and facing a 110 foot wide street is _____ feet.   17.____

    A. 178   B. 180   C. 195   D. 205

18. The MAXIMUM height of a multiple dwelling set back eight feet from the street line and facing a 90 foot wide street is _____ feet.   18.____

    A. 135   B. 147   C. 178   D. 159

Questions 19-23.

DIRECTIONS: Questions 19 through 23 are to be answered SOLELY on the basis of the following statement.

The number of persons accommodated on any story in a lodging house shall not be greater than the sum of the following components,

   a. 22 persons for each full multiple of 22 inches in the smallest clear width for each means of egress approved by the department, other than fire escapes
   b. 20 persons for each lawful fire escape accessible from such story.

19. The MAXIMUM number of persons that may be accommodated on a story in a lodging house depends on the   19.____

    A. number of lawful fire escapes *only*
    B. number of approved means of egress *only*
    C. smallest clear width in each approved means of egress *only*
    D. number of lawful fire escapes and sum total of smallest clear widths in each approved means of egress

20. The MAXIMUM number of persons that may be accommodated on a story of a lodging house having one lawful fire escape and a sum total of 44 inches in the smallest clear widths of the two approved means of egress is   20.____

    A. 20   B. 22   C. 42   D. 64

21. The MAXIMUM number of persons that may be accommodated on a story of a lodging house having two lawful fire escapes and a sum total of 60 inches in the smallest clear width of the approved means of egress is

    A. 64   B. 84   C. 100   D. 106

22. The MAXIMUM number of persons that may be accommodated on a story of a lodging house having one lawful fire escape and a sum total of 33 inches in the smallest clear width of the approved means of egress is

    A. 42   B. 53   C. 64   D. 73

23. The MAXIMUM number of persons that may be accommodated on a story of a lodging house having two lawful fire escapes and two approved means of egress, with 40 inches and 44 inches in the smallest clear widths, respectively, is

    A. 84   B. 104   C. 106   D. 108

Questions 24-25.

DIRECTIONS: Questions 24 and 25 are to be answered SOLELY on the basis of the following paragraph.

Though the recent trend toward apartment construction may appear to be the Region's response to large-lot zoning and centralized industry, it really is not. It is mainly a function of the age of the population. Most of the apartments are occupied by one- and two-person families young people out of school but without a family of their own and older people whose children have grown. Both groups have been increasing in number; and, in this Region, they characteristically live in apartments. It is this increased demand for apartments and the simultaneous decrease in demand for one-family houses that dramatically raised the percentage of building permits issued for multi-family housing units from 36 percent in 1977 to 67 percent in 1981. The fact that three-fourths of the apartments were built in the Core between 1977 and 1981 at the same time as the Core was losing population underscores the failure of the apartment boom to slow the outward spread of the population.

24. According to the above paragraph, one of the reasons for the increase in the number of building permits issued for multi-family construction in the City Metropolitan Region is

    A. that workers in industry want to live close to their jobs
    B. an increase in the number of elderly people living in the Region
    C. the inability of many families to afford the large lots necessary to build private homes
    D. the new zoning ordinance made it easier to build apartments

25. According to the above paragraph, the apartment construction boom

    A. increased the population density in the Core
    B. spurred a population shift to the suburbs
    C. did not halt the outward flow of the population from the Core
    D. was most significant in the outer areas of the Region

KEY (CORRECT ANSWERS)

1. A
2. C
3. D
4. C
5. C

6. A
7. B
8. D
9. D
10. B

11. C
12. D
13. D
14. C
15. B

16. C
17. A
18. D
19. D
20. D

21. B
22. A
23. C
24. B
25. C

TEST 2

DIRECTIONS: Each question or incomplete statement is followed by several suggested answers or completions. Select the one that BEST answers the question or completes the statement. *PRINT THE LETTER OF THE CORRECT ANSWER IN THE SPACE AT THE RIGHT.*

Questions 1-4.

DIRECTIONS: Questions 1 through 4 are to be answered SOLELY on the basis of the following paragraph.

Although the suburbs have provided housing and employment for millions of additional families since 1950, many suburban communities have maintained controls over the kinds of families who can live in them. Suburban attitudes have been formed by reaction against a perception of crowded, harassed city life and threatening alien city people. As population, taxable income, and jobs have left the cities for the suburbs, the *urban crisis* of substandard housing, declining levels of education and public services, and decreasing employment opportunities has been created. The crisis, however, is not urban at all, but national, and in part a result of the suburban policy that discourages outward movement by the urban poor.

1. According to the above paragraph, the quality of urban life

    A. is determined by public opinion in the cities
    B. has worsened in recent years
    C. is similar to rural life
    D. can be changed by political means

2. According to the above paragraph, suburban communities have

    A. tried to show that the urban crisis is really a national crisis
    B. avoided taking a position on the urban crisis
    C. been involved in causing the urban crisis
    D. been the innocent victims of the urban crisis

3. According to the above paragraph, the poor have

    A. become increasingly sophisticated in their attempts to move to the suburbs
    B. generally been excluded from the suburbs
    C. lost incentive for betterment of their living conditions
    D. sought improvement of the central cities

4. As used in the above paragraph, the word perception means MOST NEARLY

    A. development   B. impression
    C. opposition   D. uncertainty

Questions 5-8.

DIRECTIONS: Questions 5 through 8 are to be answered SOLELY on the basis of the following paragraph.

The concentration of publicly assisted housing in central cities -- because the suburbs do not want them and effectively bar them -- is usually rationalized by a solicitous regard for keeping intact the city neighborhoods cherished by low-income groups. If one accepted this as valid, the devotion of minorities to blighted city neighborhoods in preference to suburban employment and housing would be an historic first. Certainly no such devotion was visible among the millions who have deserted their city neighborhoods in the last 25 years even if it meant an arduous daily trip from the suburbs to their jobs in the cities.

5. The writer implies that MOST poor people

    A. prefer isolation
    B. fear change
    C. are angry
    D. seek betterment

6. The general tone of the paragraph is BEST characterized as

    A. uncertain   B. skeptical   C. evasive   D. indifferent

7. As used in the above paragraph, the word rationalize means MOST NEARLY

    A. dispute   B. justify   C. deny   D. locate

8. According to the above paragraph, publicly assisted housing is concentrated in the central cities PRIMARILY because

    A. city dwellers are unable to find satisfactory housing
    B. deterioration of older housing has increased in recent years
    C. suburbanites have opposed the movement of the poor to the suburbs
    D. employment opportunities have decreased in the suburbs

Questions 9-11.

DIRECTIONS: Questions 9 through 11 are to be answered SOLELY on the basis of the following paragraph.

In recent years, new and important emphasis has been placed upon the maximum use of conservation and rehabilitation techniques in carrying out programs of urban renewal and revitalization. In urban renewal projects where existing structures are hopelessly deteriorated or land uses are incompatible with the community's overall plans, the entire area may be acquired, cleared, and sold for redevelopment. However, where existing structures are basically sound but have deteriorated to the point where they are a blighting influence on the neighborhood, they may be salvaged through a program of rehabilitation and reconditioning.

9. According to the above paragraph, the one of the following which is MOST likely to cause area-wide razing of the buildings in urban renewal programs is

    A. a program of rehabilitation and reconditioning
    B. concerted insistence by landlords and tenants that certain buildings be bulldozed
    C. an inability of community groups to agree on priorities for staged clearance
    D. land use contrary to the community's general plan

10. According to the above paragraph, rehabilitation of structures may take place if

    A. new conservation and rehabilitation techniques are used
    B. salvaging all the buildings in the entire area is hopeless
    C. the community wishes to preserve historic structures
    D. the existing buildings are structurally sound

11. As used in the above paragraph, the word <u>blighting</u> means MOST NEARLY   11._____

    A. ruining   B. infrequent   C. recurrent   D. traditional

Questions 12-13.

DIRECTIONS: Questions 12 and 13 are to be answered SOLELY on the basis of the following paragraphs.

We must also find better ways to handle the relocation of people uprooted by projects. In the past, many renewal plans have foundered on this problem, and it is still the most difficult part of the community development. Large-scale replacement of low-income residents -- many ineligible for public housing -- has contributed to deterioration of surrounding communities. However, thanks to changes in housing authority procedures, relocation has been accomplished in a far more satisfactory fashion. The step-by-step community development projects we advocate in this plan should bring further improvement.

But additional measures will be necessary. There are going to be more people to be moved; and, with the current shortage of apartments, large ones especially, it is going to be tougher to find places to move them to. The city should have more freedom to buy or lease housing that comes on the market because of normal turnover and make it available to relocatees.

12. According to the above paragraphs, one of the reasons a neighborhood may deteriorate is that   12._____

    A. there is a scarcity of large apartments
    B. step-by-step community development projects have failed
    C. people in the given neighborhood are uprooted from their homes
    D. a nearby renewal project has an inadequate relocation plan

13. From the above paragraphs, one might conclude that the relocation phase of community renewal has been improved.   13._____

    A. by changes in housing authority procedures
    B. by development of step-by-step community development projects
    C. through expanded city powers to buy housing for relocation
    D. by the addition of huge sums of money

Questions 14-15.

DIRECTIONS: Questions 14 and 15 are to be answered SOLELY on the basis of the following paragraphs.

Provision of decent housing for the lower half of the population (by income) was thus taken on as a public responsibility. Public housing was to assist the poorest quarter of urban families while the 221(d)(3) Housing Program would assist the next quarter. But limited funds meant that the supply of subsidized housing could not stretch nearly far enough to help this half of the population. Who were to be left out in the rationing process which was accomplished by the sifting of applicants for housing on the part of public and private authorities?

Discrimination on the grounds of race or color is not allowed under Federal law. In all sections of the country, encouragingly, housing programs are found which follow this law to the letter. Yet, housing programs in some cities still suffer from the residue of racial segregation policies and attitudes that for years were condoned or even encouraged.

Some sifting in the 221(d)(3) Housing Program follows the practice of many public housing authorities, the imposition of requirements with respect to character. This is a delicate matter. To fill a project overwhelmingly with broken families, alcoholics, criminals, delinquents, and other problem tenants would hardly make it a wholesome environment. Yet the total exclusion of such families is hardly an acceptable alternative. To the extent this exclusion is practiced, the very people whose lives are described in order to persuade lawmakers and the public to instigate new programs find the door shut in their faces when such programs come into being. The proper balance is difficult to achieve, but society's neediest families surely should not be totally denied the opportunities for rejuvenation in subsidized housing.

14. From the above paragraphs, it can be assumed that the 221(d)(3) Housing Program

    A. served a population earning more than the median income
    B. served a less affluent population than is served by public housing
    C. excludes all problem families from its projects
    D. is a subsidized housing program

15. According to this text, the provision of housing for the poor

    A. has not been completely accomplished with public monies
    B. is never influenced by segregationist policies
    C. is limited to providing housing for only the neediest families
    D. is primarily the responsibility of the Federal government

16. Five hundred persons attended a public hearing at which a proposed public housing project was being considered. Less than half favored the project while the majority opposed the project.
    According to the above statement, it is REASONABLE to conclude that

    A. the proposal stimulated considerable community interest
    B. the public housing project was disapproved by the city because a majority opposed it
    C. those who opposed the project lacked sympathy for needy persons
    D. the supporters of the project were led by militants

17. A vacant lot close to a polluted creek is for sale. Two buyers compete. One owns an adjacent factory which provides 300 high paying unskilled jobs. He needs to expand or move from the city. If he expands, he will provide 300 additional jobs. The other is a community group in a changing residential area close by. They hope to stabilize the neighborhood by bringing in new housing. They would build an apartment building with 100 dwelling units on the lot.
    According to the above paragraph, it is REASONABLE to conclude that

    A. jobs are more important than housing
    B. there is conflict between the factory owners and the neighborhood group
    C. the neighborhood group will not succeed in stabilizing the area by constructing new housing
    D. the polluted creek should be cleaned up

18. The housing authority faces every problem of the private developer, and it must also assume responsibilities of which private building is free. The authority must account to the community; it must conform to federal regulations; it must provide durable buildings of good standard at low cost; it must overcome the prejudices against public operations, of contractors, bankers, and prospective tenants. These authorities are being watched by anti-housing enthusiasts for the first error of judgment or the first evidence of high costs, to be torn to bits before a Congressional committee.
On the basis of this statement, it would be MOST correct to state that

18.____

   A. private builders do not have the opposition of contractors, bankers, and prospective tenants
   B. Congressional committees impede the progress of public housing by petty investigations
   C. a housing authority must deal with all the difficulties encountered by the private builder
   D. housing authorities are no more immune from errors in judgment than private developers

19. Another factor that has considerably added to the city's housing crisis has been the great influx of low-income workers and their families seeking better employment opportunities during wartime and defense boom periods. The circumstances of these families have forced them to crowd into the worst kind of housing and have produced on a renewed scale the conditions from which slums flourish and grow.
On the basis of this statement, one would be justified in stating that

19.____

   A. the influx of low-income workers has aggravated the slum problem
   B. the city has better employment opportunities than other sections of the country
   C. the high wages paid by our defense industries have made many families ineligible for tenancy in public housing projects
   D. the families who settled in the city during wartime and the defense build-up brought with them language and social customs conducive to the growth of slums

20. Much of the city felt the effects of the general postwar increase of vandalism and street crime, and the greatly expanded public housing program was no exception. Projects built in congested slum areas with a high incidence of delinquency and crime were particularly subjected to the depredations of neighborhood gangs. The civil service watchmen who patrolled the projects, unarmed and neither trained nor expected to perform police duties, were unable to cope with the situation.
On the basis of this statement, the MOST accurate of the following statements is:

20.____

   A. Neighborhood gangs were particularly responsible for the high incidence of delinquency and crime in congested slum areas having public housing programs
   B. Civil service watchmen who patrolled housing projects failed to carry out their assigned police duties
   C. Housing projects were not spared the effects of the general postwar increase of vandalism and street crime
   D. Delinquency and crime affected housing projects in slum areas to a greater extent than other dwellings in the same area

21. Another peculiar characteristic of real estate is the absence of liquidity. Each parcel is a discrete unit as to size, location, rental, physical condition, and financing arrangements. Each property requires investigation, comparison of rents with other properties, and individualized haggling on price and terms.
On the basis of this statement, the LEAST accurate of the following statements is:

    A. Although the size, location, and rent of parcels vary, comparison with rents of other properties affords an indication of the value of a particular parcel
    B. Bargaining skill is the essential factor in determining the value of a parcel of real estate
    C. Each parcel of real estate has individual peculiarities distinguishing it from any other parcel
    D. Real estate is not easily converted to other types of assets

21._____

22. In part, at least, the charges of sameness, monotony, and institutionalism directed at public housing projects result from the degree in which they differ from the city's normal housing pattern. They seem alike because their very difference from the usual makes them stand apart.
In many respects, there is considerably more variety between public housing projects than there is between different streets of apartment houses or tenements throughout the city.
On the basis of this statement, it would be LEAST accurate to state that:

    A. There is considerably more variety between public housing projects than there is between different streets of tenements throughout the city
    B. Public housing projects differ from the city's normal housing pattern to the degree that sameness, monotony, and institutionalism are characteristic of public buildings
    C. Public housing projects seem alike because their deviation from the usual dwellings draws attention to them
    D. The variety in structure between public housing projects and other public buildings is related to the period in which they were built

22._____

23. The amount of debt that can be charged against the city for public housing is limited by law. Part of the city's restricted housing means goes for cash subsidies it may be required to contribute to state-aided projects. Under the provisions of the state law, the city must match the state's contributions in subsidies; and while the value of the partial tax exemption granted by the city is counted for this purpose, it is not always sufficient.
On the basis of this statement, it would be MOST accurate to state that:

    A. The amount of money the city may spend for public housing is limited by annual tax revenues
    B. The value of tax exemptions granted by the city to educational, religious, and charitable institutions may be added to its subsidy contributions to public housing projects
    C. The subsidy contributions for state-aided public housing projects are shared equally by the state and the city under the provisions of the state law
    D. The tax revenues of the city, unless supplemented by state aid, are insufficient to finance public housing projects

23._____

24. Maintenance costs can be minimized and the useful life of houses can be extended by building with the best and most permanent materials available. The best and most permanent materials in many cases are, however, much more expensive than materials which require more maintenance. The most economical procedure in home building has been to compromise between the capital costs of high quality and enduring materials and the maintenance costs of less desirable materials.
On the basis of this statement, one would be justified in stating that:

   A. Savings in maintenance costs make the use of less durable and less expensive building materials preferable to high quality materials that would prolong the useful life of houses constructed from them
   B. Financial advantage can be secured by the home builder if he judiciously combines costly but enduring building materials with less desirable materials which, however, require more maintenance
   C. A compromise between the capital costs of high quality materials and the maintenance costs of less desirable materials makes it easier for a home builder to estimate construction expenditures
   D. The most economical procedure in home building is to balance the capital costs of the most permanent materials against the costs of less expensive materials that are cheaper to maintain

24.____

25. Personnel selection has been a critical problem for local housing authorities. The pool of qualified workers trained in housing procedures is small, and the colleges and universities have failed to grasp the opportunity for enlarging it. While real estate experience makes a good background for management of a housing project, many real estate men are deplorably lacking in understanding of social and governmental problems. Social workers, on the other hand, are likely to be deficient in business judgment.
On the basis of this statement, it would be MOST accurate to state that:

   A. Colleges and universities have failed to train qualified workers for proficiency in housing procedures
   B. Social workers are deficient in business judgment as related to the management of a housing project
   C. Real estate experience makes a person a good manager of a housing project
   D. Local housing authorities have been critical of present methods of personnel selection

25.____

KEY (CORRECT ANSWERS)

1.	B	11.	A
2.	C	12.	D
3.	B	13.	A
4.	B	14.	D
5.	D	15.	A
6.	B	16.	A
7.	B	17.	B
8.	D	18.	C
9.	D	19.	A
10.	D	20.	C

21. B
22. B
23. C
24. B
25. A

GRAPHS, MAPS, SKETCHES

EXAMINATION SECTION
TEST 1

DIRECTIONS: Each question or incomplete statement is followed by several suggested answers or completions. Select the one that BEST answers the question or completes the statement. *PRINT THE LETTER OF THE CORRECT ANSWER IN THE SPACE AT THE RIGHT.*

Questions 1-7.

DIRECTIONS: Questions 1 to 7, inclusive, are based on information contained on Chart A.

1. Puritan Ricans were the LARGEST number of people in 1.____

    A. 1975   B. 1973   C. 1979   D. 1971

2. At some time between 1974 and 1975, two groups had the same number of persons. These two groups were 2.____

    A. Puerto Rican and Black
    B. Caucasian and Black
    C. Oriental and Black
    D. Puerto Rican and Caucasian

3. In the same year that the Black population reached its GREATEST peak, the LOWEST number of people residing in Revere were of the following group or groups: 3.____

    A. Puerto Rican and Caucasian
    B. Oriental
    C. Puerto Rican
    D. Puerto Rican and Oriental

4. The group which showed the GREATEST increase in population from 1970 to 1979 is 4.____

    A. Puerto Rican
    B. Caucasian
    C. Oriental
    D. not determinable from the graph

5. In 1977, the Black population was higher by APPROXIMATELY 20% over 5.____

    A. 1972   B. 1976   C. 1974   D. 1978

6. The SMALLEST number of people in 1973 were 6.____

    A. Puerto Rican and Black
    B. Oriental and Black
    C. Puerto Rican and Caucasian
    D. Puerto Rican and Oriental

7. The percent increase in population of Puerto Ricans from 1971 to 1978 is *most nearly* 7.____

   A. 34% B. 18% C. 62% D. 80%

CHART A

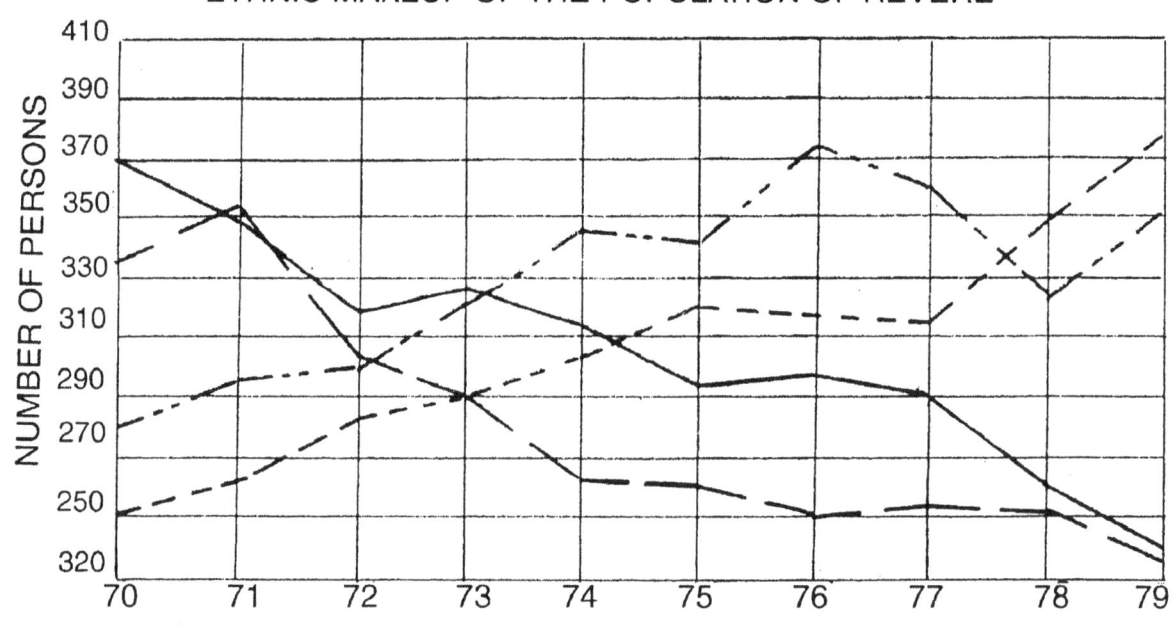

KEY (CORRECT ANSWERS)

1. C
2. D
3. B
4. A
5. A
6. D
7. A

TEST 2

DIRECTIONS: Each question or incomplete statement is followed by several suggested answers or completions. Select the one that BEST answers the question or completes the statement. *PRINT THE LETTER OF THE CORRECT ANSWER IN THE SPACE AT THE RIGHT.*

Questions 1-2.

DIRECTIONS: Questions 1 and 2 are based on information contained on Chart B.

1. The percent of Black middle students attending overcrowded schools in the period 1967 to 1968 is *most nearly*

    A. 34.6   B. 37.6   C. 44.0   D. 47.5

    1.____

2. The percent growth in total school enrollment between 1960-61 and 1967-68 is *most nearly*

    A. 37.6
    B. 45.7
    C. 35.8
    D. cannot be determined from data given

    2.____

CHART B

Summary: School Utilization and Enrollment

PRIMARY SCHOOLS	1960-61		1967-68	
NUMBER OF / PERCENT SCHOOLS / UTILIZATION	20/105		20/102	
ENROLLMENT/CAPACITY	16685/15842		18204/17813	
UTILIZATION: OVER/UNDER	NET +1942/-1099		NET +2045/-1654	
	NO. +843		NO. +391	
		%		%
WHITE ENROLLMENT	3645	21.8	3146	17.2
NEGRO ENROLLMENT	12691	76.1	14304	78.5
PUERTO RICAN ENROLLMENT	349	2.1	754	4.1

MIDDLE SCHOOLS	1960-61		1967-68	
NUMBER OF / PERCENT SCHOOLS / UTILIZATION	3/101		5/96	
ENROLLMENT/CAPACITY	4869/4808		7502/7811	
UTILIZATION: OVER/UNDER	NET +4235/-174		NET +276/-585	
	NO. +61		NO. -309	
		%		%
WHITE ENROLLMENT	1478	30.4	1717	22.8
NEGRO ENROLLMENT	3279	67.3	5228	69.6
PUERTO RICAN ENROLLMENT	112	2.3	557	7.4

HIGH SCHOOLS	1960-61		1967-68	
NUMBER OF / PERCENT SCHOOLS / UTILIZATION	2/78		3/107	
ENROLLMENT/CAPACITY	1791/2300		6003/5847	
UTILIZATION: OVER/UNDER	NET +15/-224		NET +985/-829	
	NO. -209		NO. +156	
		%		%
WHITE ENROLLMENT	1106	61.8	3266	54.4
NEGRO ENROLLMENT	650	36.3	2561	42.6
PUERTO RICAN ENROLLMENT	35	2.0	176	2.9

Detail: School Utilization and Enrollment 1967-1968

PRIMARY SCHOOLS	CONSTRUCTION— DATES AND TYPE*	GRADES	AVERAGE YRS OVER OR UNDER GRADE	SPECIAL PROGRMS	ENROLLMENT TOTAL	WHITE NO	%	NEGRO NO	%	PUERTO RICAN NO	%	CAPACITY TOTAL	AVAIL— SHORT+	% OF UTIL	OTHER UTIL ROOMS
PS 15	1939	K-5	-.1	T,AS	565	2	.3	523	92.5	40	7.0	669	+ 104	84.4	
PS 30	1965	K-5	+1.2	T,AS	1605	854	53.2	748	46.6	3	.1	1099	- 506	146.0	18 (NOTE M)
PS 35	1931	K-5	+.6	AS	640	345	53.9	259	40.4	36	5.6	702	+ 62	91.1	6 PORTABLES
PS 36	1924,63	K-5	-.3	SS	703	9	1.2	684	97.2	10	1.4	509	- 194	138.1	
PS 37	1928	K-5	+.7	MES,AS	615	61	9.9	544	88.4	10	1.6	419	- 196	146.7	
PS 40	1912,42,64	K-5	-.8	SS,MES	1058	9	.7	994	93.9	55	5.1	869	- 189	121.7	6 (NOTE N)
PS 45	1914,28,63	K-5	-.6	SS	986	7	.7	949	96.2	30	3.0	856	- 130	115.1	6 PORTABLES
PS 48	1936	K-5	+1.2	SP	495	10	2.0	482	97.3	3	.6	632	+ 137	78.3	1 (NOTE O)
PS 50	1922	K-5	-1.2	SS	772	116	15.0	593	76.8	63	8.1	833	+ 61	92.6	
PS 80	1964	K-5	+.5	T,AS	1052	421	40.0	574	54.5	57	5.4	1197	+ 145	87.8	
PS 82	1906	K-5	-1.1		440	375	85.2	21	4.7	44	10.0	378	- 62	116.4	2 (NOTE P)
PS 95	1915,25	K-5	-.1	SS	1274	489	38.3	647	50.7	138	10.8	1320	+ 46	96.5	
PS 116	1925,64	K-5	-1.4	SS	914	2	.2	902	98.6	10	1.0	1067	+ 153	85.6	
PS 118	1923,32	K-5	+.5	T	887	28	3.1	832	93.7	27	1.0	1089	+ 202	81.4	
PS 123	1926,32,64	K-5	-1.2	SS	1565	41	2.6	1448	92.5	76	4.8	1103	- 462	141.8	17 PORTABLES
PS 134	1928,38	K-5	-.3	T	1067	42	3.9	959	89.8	66	6.1	761	- 306	140.2	
PS 136	1928,37	K-5	-.9	T	987	10	1.0	950	96.2	27	2.7	1301	+ 314	75.8	1 (NOTE Q)
PS 140	1929,38,63	K-5	-.8	SS	1160	46	3.9	1098	94.6	16	1.3	1241	+ 81	93.4	
PS 160	1939	K-5	-.6	SS	1019	11	1.0	1006	98.7	2	.1	1030	+ 11	98.9	
PS 178	1951	K-5	+1.8		400	268	67.0	91	22.7	41	10.2	738	+ 338	54.2	
TOTAL PRIMARY SCHOOLS= 20					18204	3146	17.2	14304	78.5	754	4.1	17813	+ 2045 / - 1654	102.1	

MIDDLE SCHOOLS															
IS 8	1963	6-8	-.5	SS,PI	1562	325	20.8	1124	71.9	113	7.2	1523	+ 39	102.5	
IS 59	1956	6-8	-.1	PI,T,AS	1633	621	38.0	846	51.8	166	10.1	1396	- 237	116.9	
IS 72	1967	6-8		T,AS	1396	210	15.0	1171	83.8	15	1.1	1145	- 251	84.7	
IS 142	1930,38	6-8	-1.5	SS	1096	21	1.9	1004	91.6	71	6.4	1333	+ 237	82.2	
JS 192	1963	7-9	-.8		1815	540	29.7	1083	59.6	192	10.5	1912	+ 97	94.9	
TOTAL MIDDLE SCHOOLS= 5					7502	1717	22.8	5228	69.6	557	7.4	7811	+ 276 / - 585	96.0	

HIGH SCHOOLS															
SPRINGFLD GDNS	1965	9-12	-.3		4277	2758	64.4	1462	34.1	57	1.3	3292	+ 985	129.9	
JAMAICA VOC	1896-C	9-12	-2.9		644	382	59.3	235	36.4	27	4.1	895	+ 251	71.9	
W WILSON VOC	1942	9-12	-3.7		1082	126	11.6	864	79.8	92	8.5	1660	+ 578	65.1	
TOTAL HIGH SCHOOLS= 3					6003	3266	54.4	2561	42.6	176	2.9	5847	+ 985 / - 829	102.6	

NOTES
1. INCLUDES ENROLLMENT AND CAPACITY AT ANNEX (PS 170) IN QUEENS PLANNING DISTRICT 8
* EXCEPT AS NOTED ALL SCHOOLS ARE OF FIREPROOF CONSTRUCTION
C: NOT FIREPROOF
X: NOT AVAILABLE

CODE
T: TRANSITIONAL SCHOOL
AS: AFTER SCHOOL STUDY CENTER
SS: SPECIAL SERVICE SCHOOL
MES: MORE EFFECTIVE SCHOOL
SP: SPECIAL PRIMARY SCHOOL
PI: PILOT INTERMEDIATE SCHOOL

NOTES
M: IN ROCHDALE VILLAGE
N: 4 PORTABLES, 2 IN UNION METHODIST CHURCH
O: IN BROOKS MEMORIAL METHODIST CHURCH
P: AT 139-35 88TH STREET
Q: IN GRACE METHODIST EPISCOPAL CHURCH

KEY (CORRECT ANSWERS)

1. B
2. C

TEST 3

DIRECTIONS: Each question or incomplete statement is followed by several suggested answers or completions. Select the one that BEST answers the question or completes the statement. *PRINT THE LETTER OF THE CORRECT ANSWER IN THE SPACE AT THE RIGHT.*

Questions 1-4.

DIRECTIONS: Questions 1 to 4, inclusive, are based on the information contained on Chart C.

1. What percent of all households in 1960 are Puerto Rican households with incomes of $6,000 or more per year?   1.____

   A. 38%   B. 57%   C. 6%   D. 0.6%

2. The median income in all households in 1960 is in the range of   2.____

   A. $3,000 - $5,999
   B. $6,000 - $9,999
   C. $10,000 - $14,999
   D. cannot be determined from data given

3. The total number of white persons living in one or two person households in 1960 is   3.____

   A. 13,126   B. 28,884   C. 24,704   D. 46.5

4. Which of the following statements is MOST likely to be true?   4.____

   A. In 1970, the majority of the population in the above data is white.
   B. The majority of households in 1960 have incomes under $6,000.
   C. There are 8668 people in 1960 in households with incomes under $3,000.
   D. The majority of households in 1960 with incomes under $2,000 are white.

CHART C

Population and Housing Data

Housing Units

	TOTAL	1 ROOM	2 ROOMS	3 ROOMS	4 ROOMS	5 ROOMS	6+ ROOMS
TOTAL HOUSING UNITS - 1960	57611	1484	2492	10491	9074	8409	25661
TOTAL OCCUPIED HOUSING UNITS	56187						
RENTER OCCUPIED - TOTAL	23040						
PUBLIC	1048	--	44	240	553	199	12
PUBLICLY AIDED	--	--	--	--	--	--	--
OWNER OCCUPIED - TOTAL	33147						
PUBLICLY AIDED	--	--	--	--	--	--	--
PUBLIC HOUSING - 1970							
PUBLIC RENTER	1434	--	44	321	736	300	33
PUBLICLY AIDED RENTER	65	--	--	22	26	17	--
PUBLICLY AIDED OWNER	6075	--	3	2770	2214	568	520

Income 1960

	PERSONS IN HOUSEHOLD						TOTAL NUMBER OF HOUSEHOLDS
	1	2	3	4	5	6+	
WHITE HOUSEHOLDS							
UNDER $ 2000	1652	1153	276	143	122	45	3346
$ 2000 - $ 2999	459	717	176	67	58	32	1477
$ 3000 - $ 5999	1472	3018	1688	1290	944	169	8412
$ 6000 - $ 9999	501	3520	2649	2936	1900	219	10504
$10000 - $14999	75	1378	1255	1069	1144	87	4925
$15000 AND OVER	17	476	535	637	680	26	2345
NEGRO AND OTHER NON-WHITE HOUSEHOLDS							
UNDER $ 2000	464	664	366	303	444		2291
$ 2000 - $ 2999	237	453	315	192	280		1477
$ 3000 - $ 5999	587	2368	1721	1304	2313		8293
$ 6000 - $ 9999	98	1735	1984	1650	2465		7932
$10000 - $14999	13	370	547	679	1370		3025
$15000 AND OVER	--	--	82	116	435		656
PUERTO RICAN HOUSEHOLDS							
UNDER $ 2000	9	7	7	11	11		45
$ 2000 - $ 2999	4	2	2	14	12		32
$ 3000 - $ 5999	10	17	45	26	71		169
$ 6000 - $ 9999	--	42	35	30	112		219
$10000 - $14999	--	8	5	21	53		87
$15000 AND OVER	--	1	4	3	19		26
ALL HOUSEHOLDS							
UNDER $ 2000	2155	1824	649	457	577		5162
$ 2000 - $ 2999	700	1170	493	273	350		2986
$ 3000 - $ 5999	2069	5403	3454	2620	3328		16874
$ 6000 - $ 9999	599	5297	4668	4616	4477		18657
$10000 - $14999	92	1776	1857	1769	2567		8041
$15000 AND OVER	17	499	621	756	1134		3027

Population Growth

(Line graph showing population from 1950 to 1970, y-axis 0 to 250,000)

Ethnic Make-up (in percent)

White ○
Black ●
Puerto Rican ∗

Households 1960 (in percent)

% OF ALL HOUSEHOLDS

	PERSONS IN HOUSEHOLDS						
	1	2	3	4	5	6+	
White	56	14	7	23	21	17	9	7
Black	43		4	13	20	19	13	18
Puerto Rican	1				17	18	21	27
All Households	100%	12	23	20	17	12	12

KEY (CORRECT ANSWERS)

1. D
2. B
3. C
4. D

TEST 4

DIRECTIONS: Each question or incomplete statement is followed by several suggested answers or completions. Select the one that BEST answers the question or completes the statement. *PRINT THE LETTER OF THE CORRECT ANSWER IN THE SPACE AT THE RIGHT.*

Questions 1-4.

DIRECTIONS: Questions 1 through 4, inclusive, are based on information contained on Chart D.

1. The percentage of households by ethnic make-up in 1960 was *most nearly* 1._____

   A. 16% white, 12% Black and other non-white, 16% Puerto Rican, and 56% not reported
   B. 39% white, 26% Black and other non-white, and 35% Puerto Rican
   C. 95% white, 3% Black and 2% Puerto Rican
   D. 99% white, 1% Black and other non-white, and 0% Puerto Rican

2. In 1960, the predominant age group was in the age range of 2._____

   A. 5-15   B. 25-44   C. 45-64   D. 0-15

3. In 1960, the LARGEST singular and discrete income group consisted of households with the following characteristics: 3._____

   A. Black and other non-white households of 3 persons with total earnings of between $6,000 and $9,999
   B. White households with 3 persons with total earnings from under $2,000 to $5,999
   C. White households of 2 persons with total earnings between $6,000 and $9,999
   D. White households with total earnings under $2,000

4. The percent population increase between 1950 and 1970 was most nearly 4._____

   A. 56%   B. 30%   C. 25%   D. 33%

CHART D

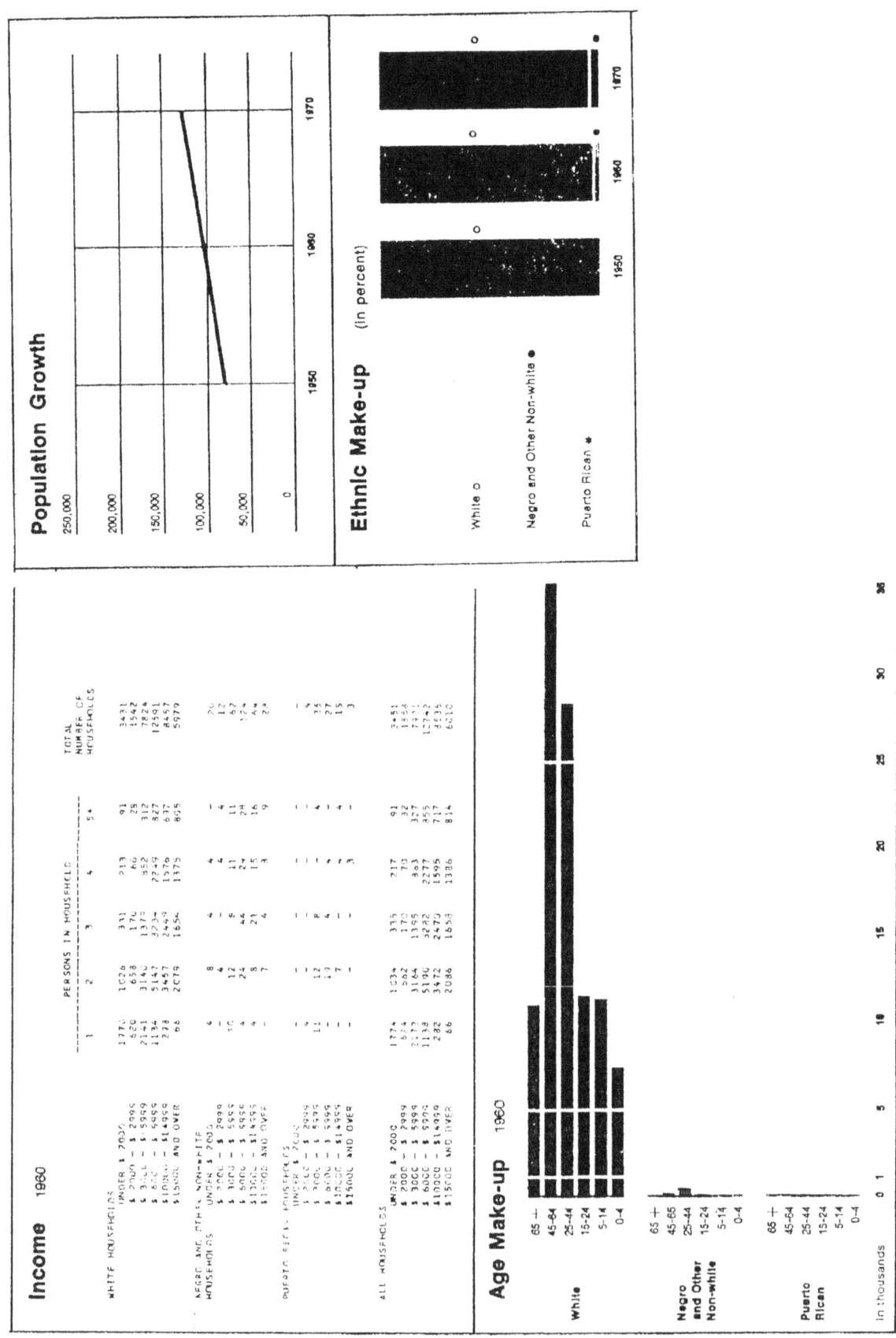

KEY (CORRECT ANSWERS)

1. D
2. C
3. C
4. A

TEST 5

DIRECTIONS: Each question or incomplete statement is followed by several suggested answers or completions. Select the one that BEST answers the question or completes the statement. *PRINT THE LETTER OF THE CORRECT ANSWER IN THE SPACE AT THE RIGHT.*

Questions 1-3.

DIRECTIONS: Questions 1 through 3, inclusive, are based on information contained on Zoning Map E. Zoning Map E is drawn to scale. Candidates are to scale off measurements.

1. One-third of Block A (shaded area) has already been developed as a public housing project. It is proposed that a second development be built on the remainder of the site. The approximate size of the proposed site, in acres, is *most nearly* (43,650 sq.ft. = 1 acre)

    A. 5.9 B. 55 C. 1.8 D. 10.3

    1.____

2. If Site B were developed for housing and 40% of the site was covered by buildings, the amount of open space would be *most nearly* _____ acres.

    A. 2.5 B. 6.3 C. 3.8 D. 2.7

    2.____

3. A new elementary school will have to be built to accommodate the children from the two proposed projects at A and B.
If the new school must be within 1/2 mile walk of any point in either project, which would be the *most likely* site?

    A. 1 B. 2 C. 3 D. 4

    3.____

2 (#5)

ZONING MAP E

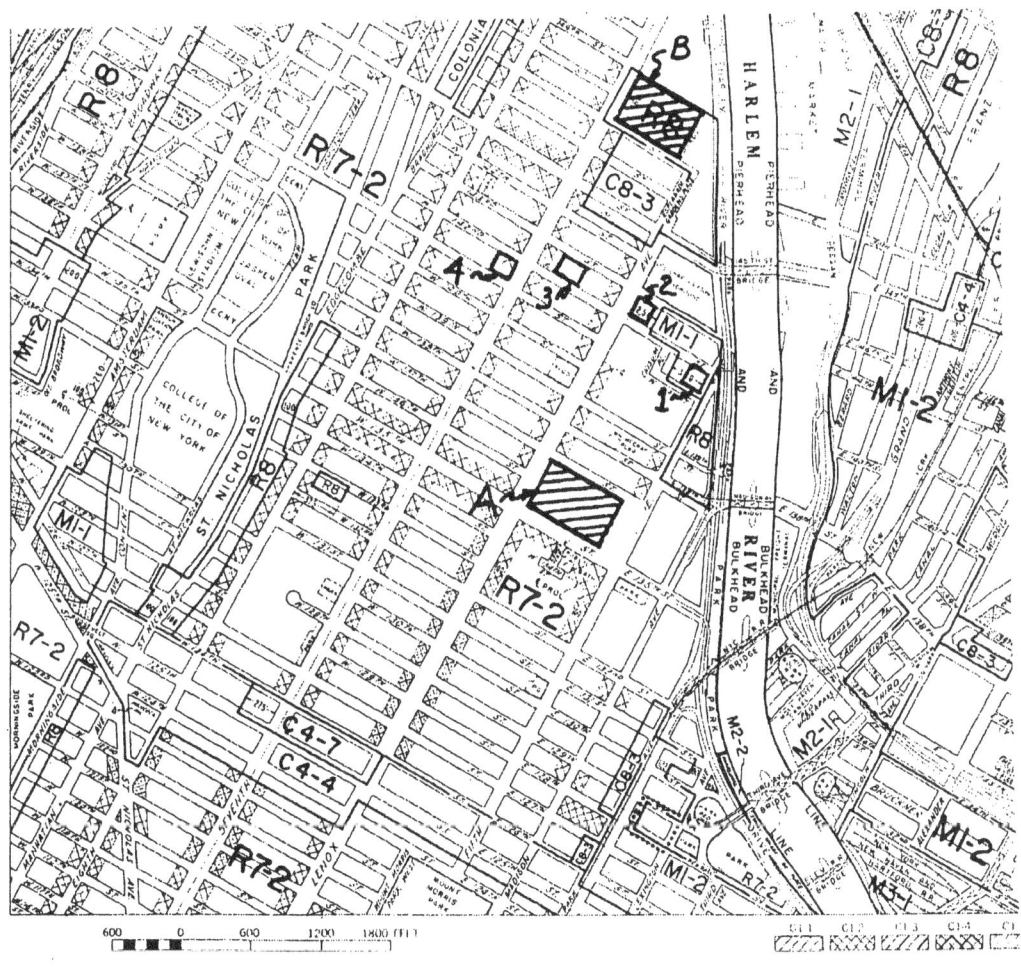

KEY (CORRECT ANSWERS)

1. A
2. C
3. B

TEST 6

DIRECTIONS: Each question or incomplete statement is followed by several suggested answers or completions. Select the one that BEST answers the question or completes the statement. *PRINT THE LETTER OF THE CORRECT ANSWER IN THE SPACE AT THE RIGHT.*

Questions 1-2.

DIRECTIONS: Questions 1 and 2 are to be answered in accordance with the Coast and Geodetic Map F.

1. The difference in elevation between the lowest and highest point of Ewen Park is *most nearly* _____ feet.   1._____

   A. 100   B. 25   C. 200   D. 50

2. Given: The scale of the map is as shown.   2._____
   The distance between the College of Mt. St. Vincent and Ewen Park is *most nearly* _____ feet.

   A. 2,000   B. 6,000   C. 24,000   D. 12,000

COAST & GEODETIC MAP F

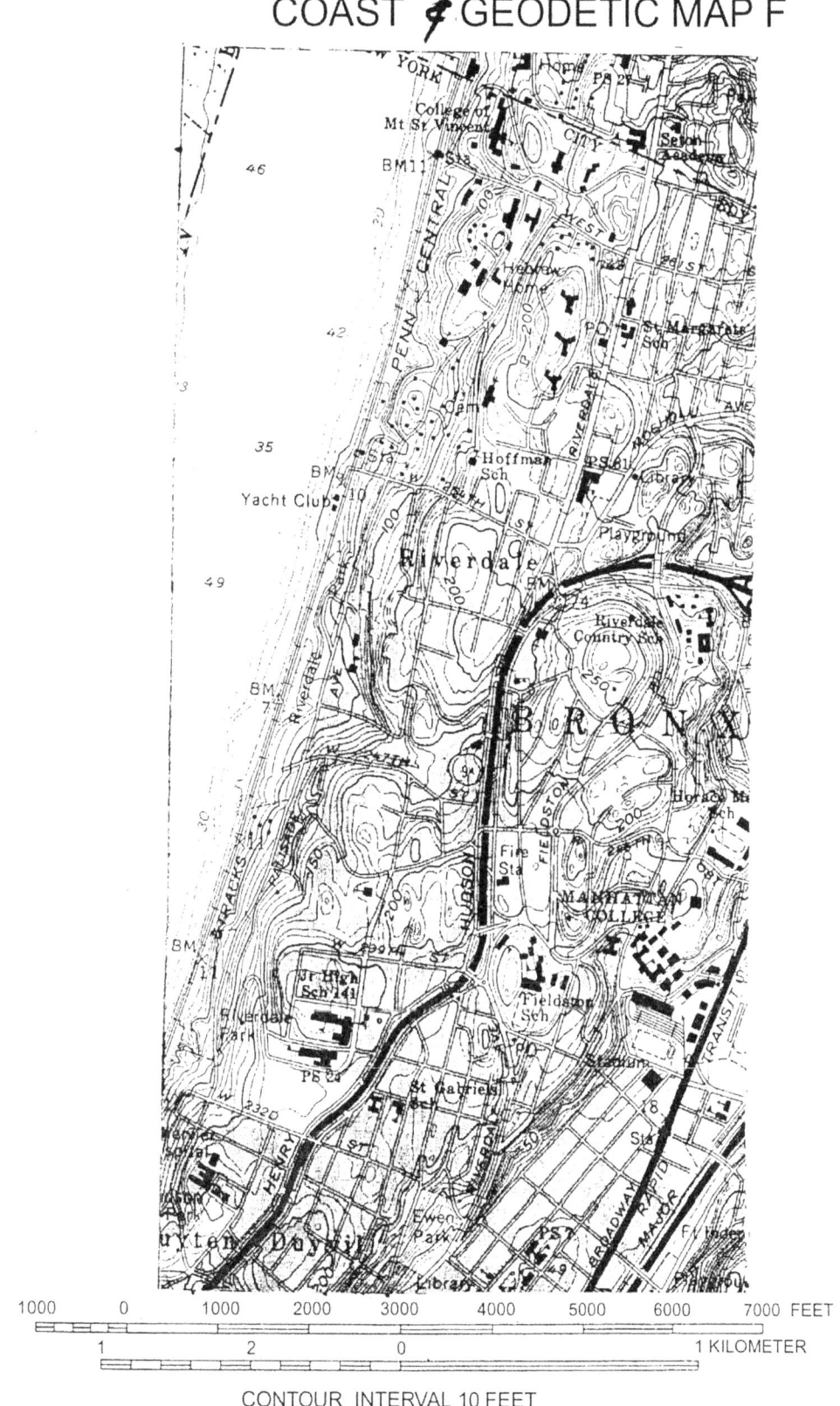

CONTOUR INTERVAL 10 FEET

KEY (CORRECT ANSWERS)

1. A
2. D

TEST 7

DIRECTIONS: Each question or incomplete statement is followed by several suggested answers or completions. Select the one that BEST answers the question or completes the statement. *PRINT THE LETTER OF THE CORRECT ANSWER IN THE SPACE AT THE RIGHT.*

Questions 1-3.

DIRECTIONS: Questions 1 to 3, inclusive, are based on information contained on Sketch G, a birds-eye view of a proposed development.

NOTE: The attached single family homes in the periphery are one-story high and contain 1,000 square feet. They are square buildings.

1. The dimension A of this single family attached home is *most nearly* _____ feet. 1._____
   A. 20 B. 32 C. 50 D. 100

2. The dimension B of the road is *most nearly* _____ feet. 2._____
   A. 25 B. 48 C. 75 D. 100

3. The dimension C of the courtyard is *most nearly* _____ feet. 3._____
   A. 40 B. 85 C. 57 D. 150

2 (#7)

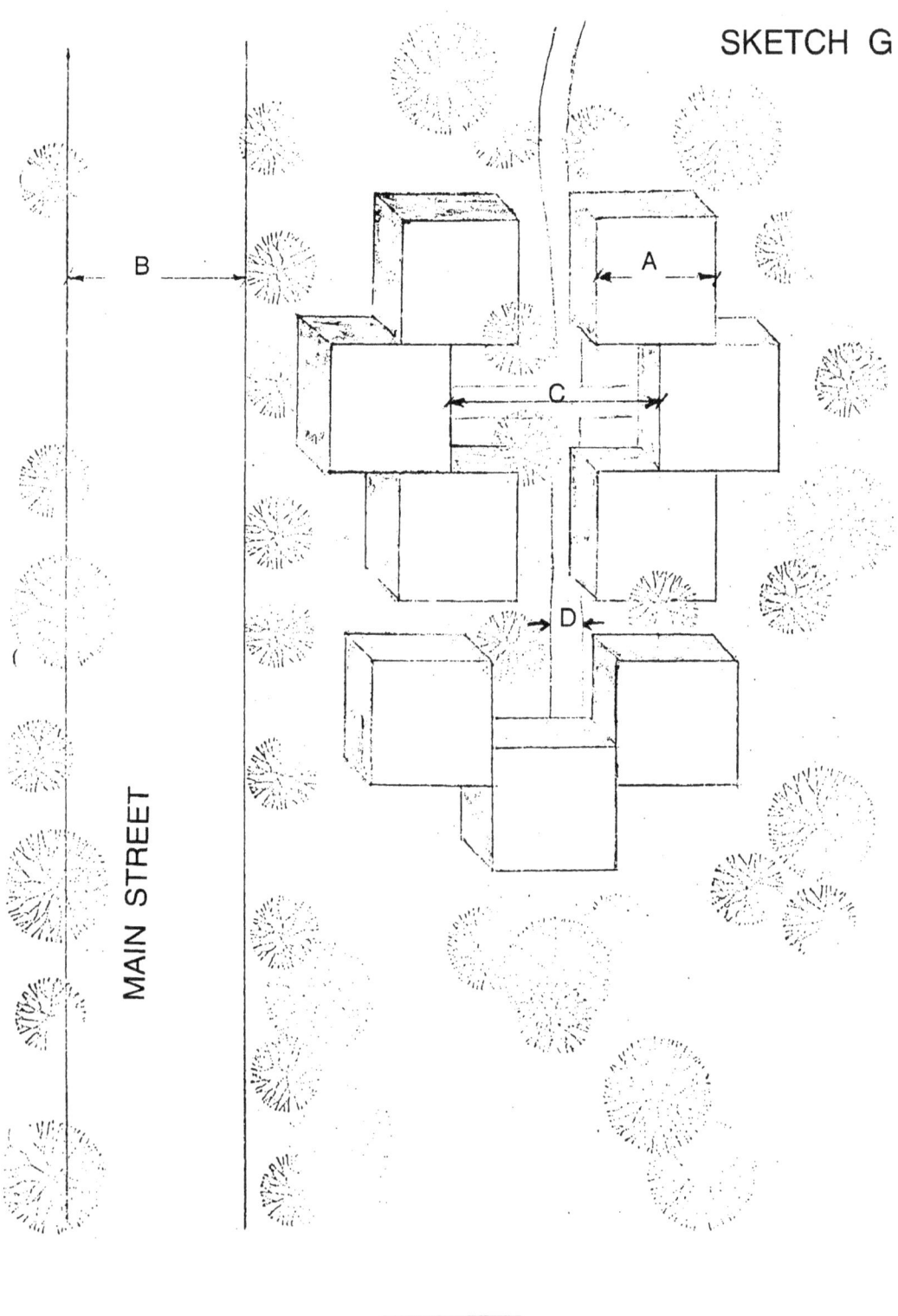

SKETCH G

KEY (CORRECT ANSWERS)

1. B
2. B
3. C

LAND DEVELOPMENT

CONTENTS

	Page
I. COMMUNITY CENTERS	1
Size	1
Location	1
Access	2
Number of access points	3
Access-point design	4
Site design	7
Parking	10
II. WORK SITES	12
Parking demand	13
Peak-hour demand	13
Site selection	13
Parking design	14

LAND DEVELOPMENT

COMMUNITY CENTERS WORK SITES

LAND DEVELOPMENT DETERMINES ROAD NEEDS

Land use, to a large extent, **determines road needs**. Therefore, any change in land use should be evaluated to determine its probable effect on the road system. The evaluation should answer two basic questions: "*Will the new development create congestion or unsafe conditions on adjacent streets?*" and "*Will the new development have adequate off-street parking?*"

Most small developments will not generate enough traffic to create capacity-related congestion. However, this may not be true for community centers, large office buildings, commissaries, exchanges, and hospitals. This chapter provides guidance for evaluating access and parking design for these facilities.

I. COMMUNITY CENTER

A community center is a group of commercial establishments planned and developed to maximize the sale of goods and provision of services. This grouping of related activities on one site, with common access and off-street parking facilities, benefits both tenants and patrons and has proved to be a successful marketing concept. However, these centers generate heavy traffic volumes, which require a sophisticated design for site access and external roadways to accommodate the traffic demand.

SIZE
On military installations, there are two basic types of centers: **neighborhood and community.** **Neighborhood centers** sell daily living needs (food, drugs, sundries, and personal services). They include from 5 to 15 stores, require at least 1,000 families for support, and need from 5 to 10 acres of land.

Community centers generally contain a major exchange, commissary, bank, credit union, theater, snack bar, cafeteria, post office, bowling alley, service station, package store, barber and beauty shops, and laundry. They usually require at least 5,000 families and a site area of 15 to 30 acres.

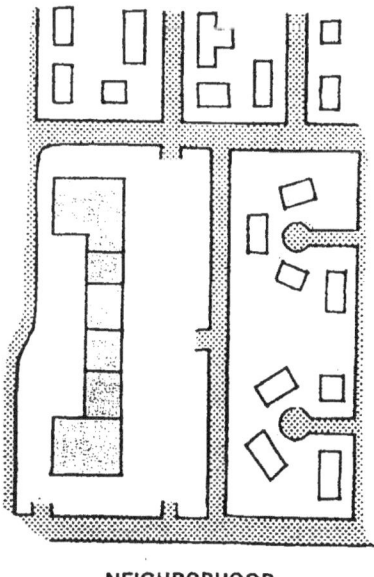

NEIGHBORHOOD

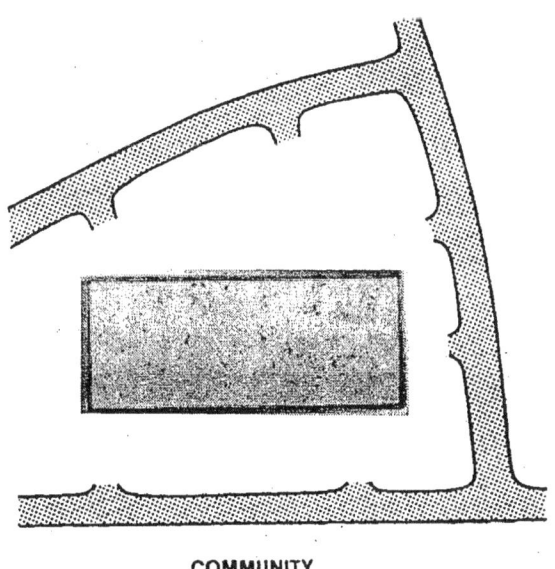

COMMUNITY

LOCATION

The **community center** should be **conveniently located with respect to a majority of its potential customers**. It should be accessible to both vehicular and pedestrian traffic; it must not be bisected by through roads.

In site selection, the land area should be large enough for proposed buildings, adequate parking facilities, and buffer zones. The site should be a single parcel, regular in shape, with generally level or gently sloping topography, safe from flooding, and without excessive drainage problems. Odd-shaped sites and rough terrain should be avoided, because they not only require contrived layouts and additional construction cost for multilevel parking areas, but they also decrease the ease of traffic circulation. Also, the land area should not require excessive fill, particularly in the area to be occupied by buildings. In every case, the bearing quality of the subsoil should be determined prior to site selection.

ACCESS

The **greatest impact of community center traffic** is generally at the site itself and on the roadways that provide direct access to the site. Therefore, analysis of traffic impact usually can be limited to the number, location, and type of access points required. A major factor in determining this requirement is the expected daily traffic pattern to and from the center. This pattern is related to the center's size, operating hours, trade area, and to patron habits.

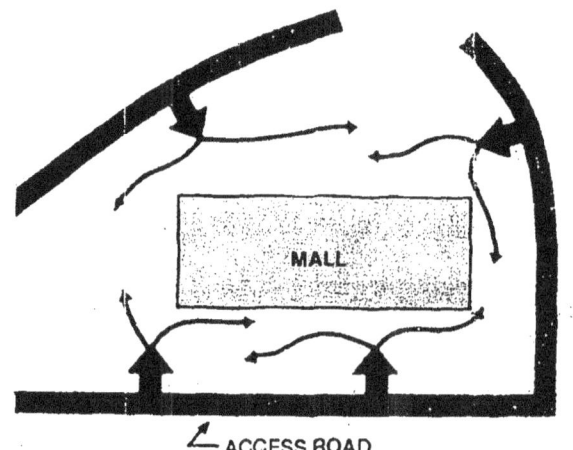

FACTORS INFLUENCING ACCESS-POINT

Amount of site frontage available for access facilities. Access to more than one major street from large centers should be provided to ensure a balanced distribution of center-generated traffic volumes.

Traffic volumes generated by the center, as well as through volumes on adjacent streets. Analysis of abutting streets for access should determine not only their ability to handle center traffic, but also the desirability of using these streets for access.

Directional distribution of center traffic approaching and departing. Unbalanced patterns are usual and should be considered when designing for turning movements.

Location and geometrics of existing cross streets and relationships to existing and future intersection spacing. If possible, existing signalized intersections should be used for access to the center. Use of these intersections can prevent possible undesirable spacing of intersections, particularly if the new access would require signalization. On the other hand, these advantages must be weighed against possible delays caused by overloading of the intersection.

Access needs of land uses adjacent to the center. When developing land around community centers, driveways for separate mall facilities (bank, service station, and so forth) should not be connected individually and directly to the major access road. If these facilities are located on the main site, the access drives should be connected to the community center internal circulation system. If they are opposite the major road providing access to the site, the drives should be aligned opposite the major community center entrances. Excessive driveways, connected individually to the access road, create traffic congestion, increase accidents, and reduce capacity. Planners should be careful not to concentrate too much activity and overload the road system.

NUMBER OF ACCESS POINTS

$$ACCESS\ DRIVES = \frac{PROJECTED\ TRIPS}{CAPACITY\ OF\ SINGLE\ ACCESS}$$

Site frontage determines the number of access points that can be provided; however, the number of access points actually provided should be based on the volume of traffic generated and the capability of each access point to serve traffic. When traffic pattern distribution is doubtful, more access points than appear to be necessary for capacity purposes should be provided.

A major factor in determining the number of access points required is the volume of traffic generated. Because of the many variables affecting traffic generation, standard rates have not been developed. However, for preliminary planning, one-way trip-generation factors of between 5 and 15 vehicle trips per hour per 1,000 square feet of gross floor area are applicable. The higher rate should be used for the smaller center and also where there is a high turnover; the lower rate is more appropriate for the larger centers. An average of 10 one-way trips per hour per 1,000 square feet of gross floor area is suggested for the average community center.

After the volume of traffic that will be generated by the center has been determined and before the number of required access points can be determined, **the capacity of a single access point must be known**. This capacity can vary widely, depending on access design, vehicle loadings, adjacent roadways, and traffic control and distribution. Criteria for determining intersection capacity, as explained in the 1965 Highway Capacity Manual, should be used for this evaluation. In this analysis, peak-hour volumes are the most critical. Peak-travel periods for most installation roadways are between 0700 and 0900 and 1600 and 1800 hours and are primarily work-related trips. Therefore, for centers that open between 0900 and 1800 hours, the peak-hour traffic may coincide with the work-related peak flows. This period would then represent the critical time frame for which street requirements should be examined and designed.

ACCESS-POINT DESIGN

The type of traffic movements to be made determines ACCESS-POINT DESIGN. In this section, typical designs for resolving access problems are shown, and design principles are given.

DESIGN GUIDES

- Access points should be designed to serve pedestrians and bicycles as well as automobiles. Many community centers are built near residential areas where non driver segments are not uncommon. Marked walkways, precautionary signing, grade-separated structures, and special crosswalk lighting are applicable protection measures for these segments.

- Driveways to handle a moderate number of left turns without signal control should have two outbound lanes; one for right turns and one for left turns. Dual turning lanes should be used only with signal control.

- Driveway cross sections may vary from a minimum one-way-in or one-way-out drive, 14 to 16 feet wide, to a maximum of four inbound and four outbound lanes. Where more than one inbound and one outbound lane is provided, a median divider at least 4 feet wide is desirable. Median widths in excess of 16 feet are generally undesirable; they create turning problems and give the access drive a larger opening on the street.

- A minimum 15-foot turning radius is essential at access points, with 25- to 50-foot radii desirable.

- Caution should be used in developing barrier channelization; too much can be a hazard.

- Basic vehicular storage requirements should be determined for each access point. On the street serving inbound traffic, left- and right-turn storage is generally critical. Inadequate storage for inbound movements will result in traffic backups onto the through lanes, reducing through-traffic capacity. For traffic exiting the center, left turns are usually the critical movement. An inadequate outbound storage lane can result in backups onto the center's internal circulation road.

TYPICAL ACCESS DESIGNS

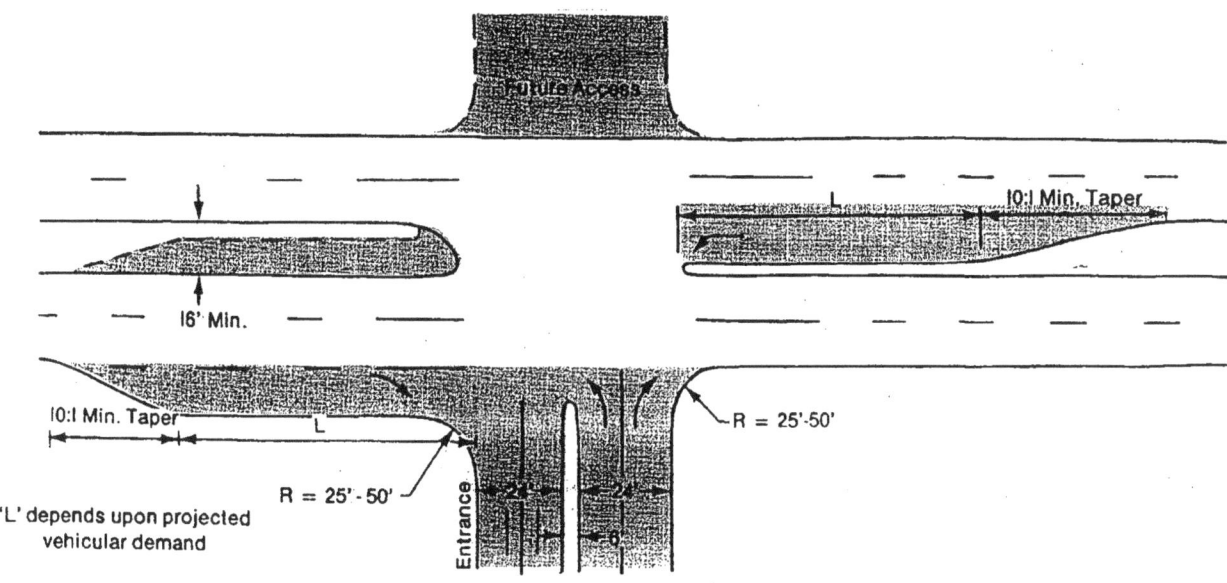

This design is the most commonly used treatment for a major entrance/exit drive. As noted in the figure, it is desirable to locate access facilities for undeveloped properties opposite the existing center's access. This allows for efficient signalization and overall safe traffic operation.

The divided cross section of the entrance provides the desired separation. As shown, the turning radii of 25 to 50 feet will permit higher turning speeds; however, if pedestrian movements are a consideration, smaller radii may be desirable. Protected left turn storage lanes are provided to separate left turning traffic from through traffic. The length of the storage lane is based on a capacity analysis. The transition taper should not be less than 10:1, and the storage lanes should be at least 12 feet wide.

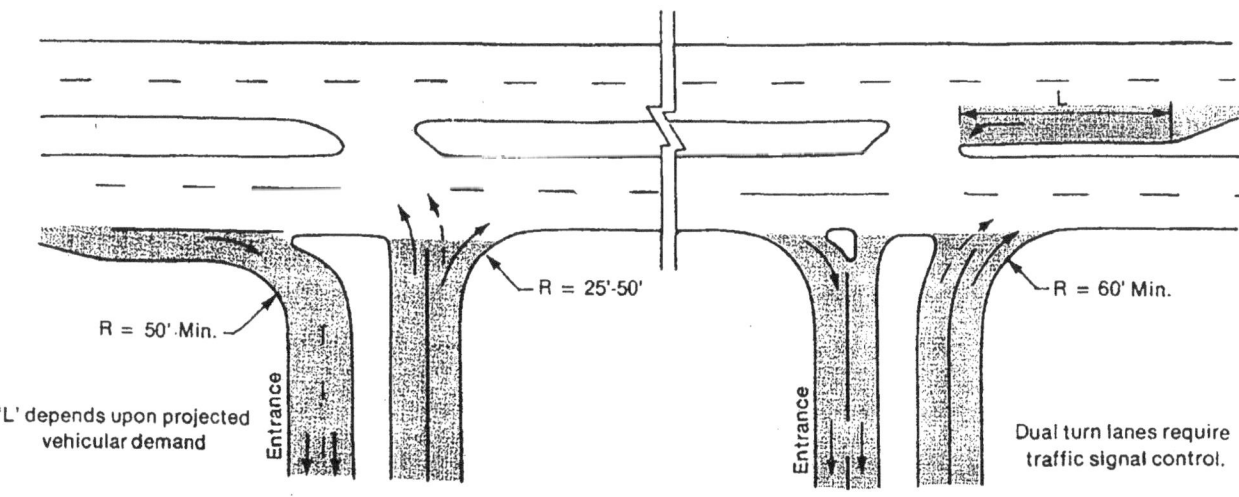

Shown in this design are directional entrance/exits that can be used for major inbound/outbound movements. The design would best serve where drivers have limited access to other entrances and thus, the use of the entrance serving each direction is maximized. Skewing of entrances can enhance operation and increase capacity.

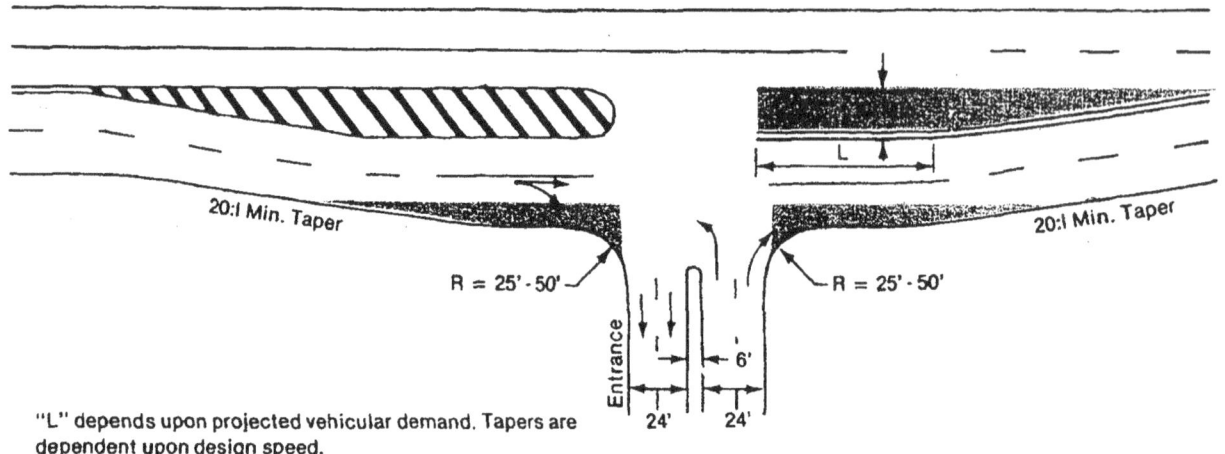

"L" depends upon projected vehicular demand. Tapers are dependent upon design speed.

Left-turn storage on an undivided route created by road widening is shown in this design. Although the roadway is shown widened on the entrance drive side, the widening may be on the opposite side or equal on both sides.

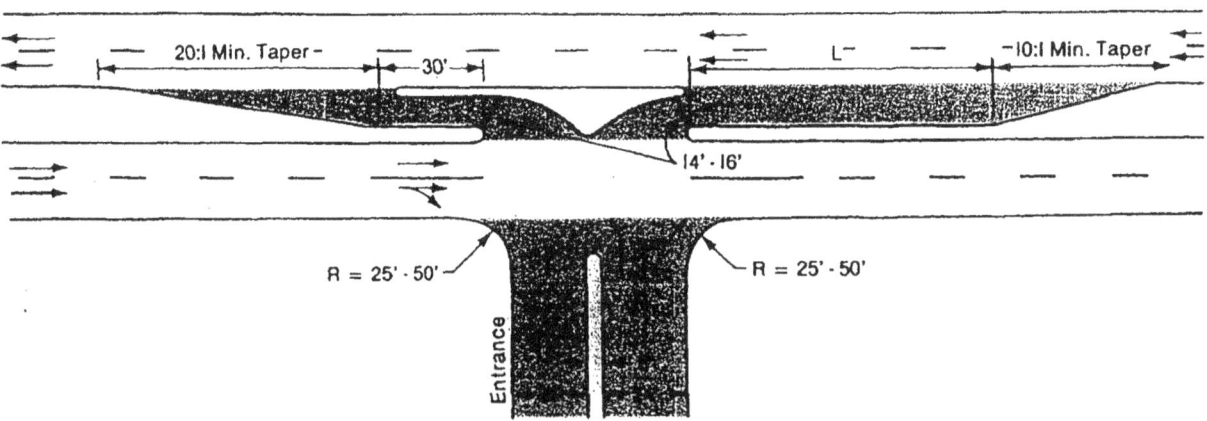

"L" depends upon projected vehicular demand. Tapers are dependent upon design speed.

This design illustrates a left-turn treatment for use on a major road with a median wider than 20 feet. It may also be used successfully on two-lane roadways where adequate width is available to flare the intersection.

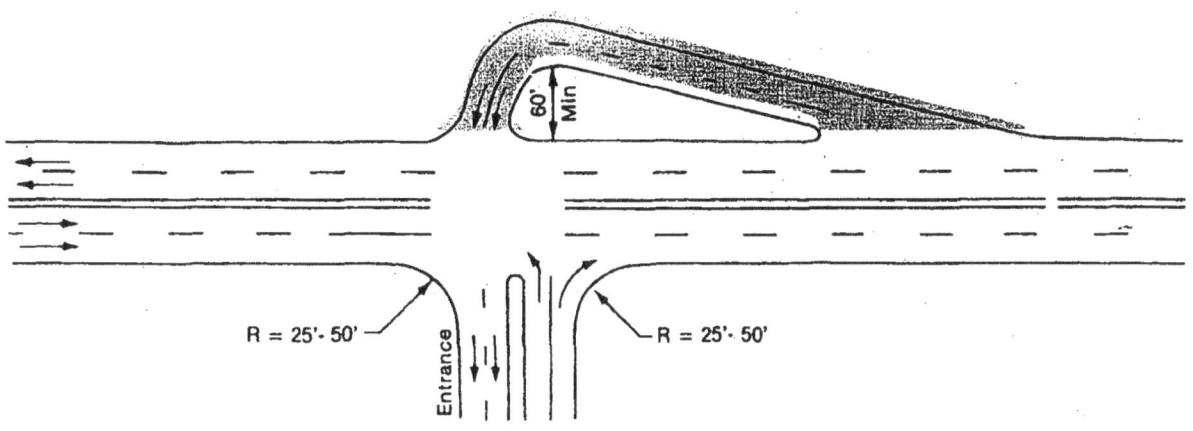

This jug handle design provides high left turn capacity and usually requires less right of way than a dual left turn

SITE DESIGN

A PRINCIPAL OBJECTIVE OF SITE DESIGN should be to bring the patron close to as many facilities as possible once the person emerges from the automobile and becomes a pedestrian.
The capability of a new development to meet this objective depends, to a large degree, on the building arrangement.

Location of buildings generally is determined by site shape, topography, access to abutting streets, use of existing structures, number and size of buildings, construction costs, and personal preference. However, **the center** generally takes one of the following forms: **strip, court, mall, or cluster**. Variations of these basic layouts can be adapted for any type of center. Usually, the strip and court layouts are most suitable for the smaller shopping centers.

BASIC SITE DESIGNS

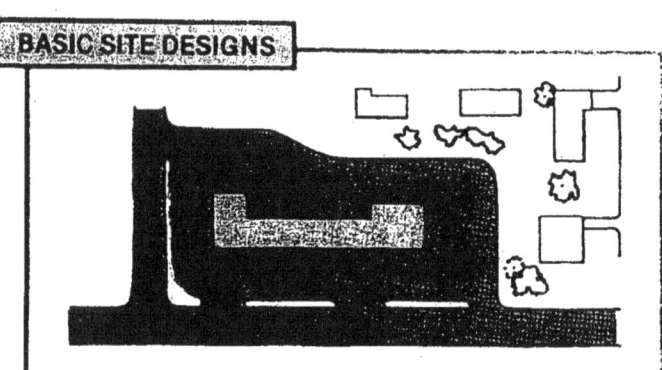

STRIP — simple lines of stores most economical for small centers.

COURT OR U — layout creates natural key store locations at ends and center, adapting to rectangular, square, or corner plots.

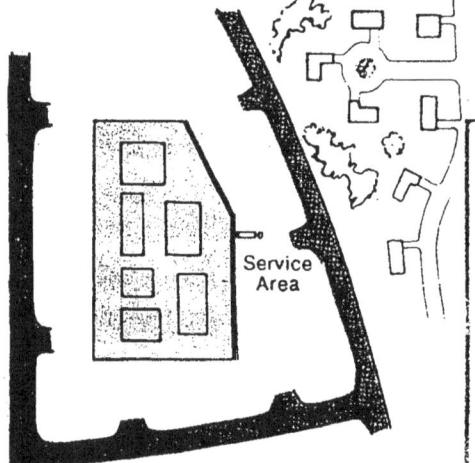

GROUP OR CLUSTER — used essentially for large centers and, with careful planning, can produce an integrated center on nearly any property.

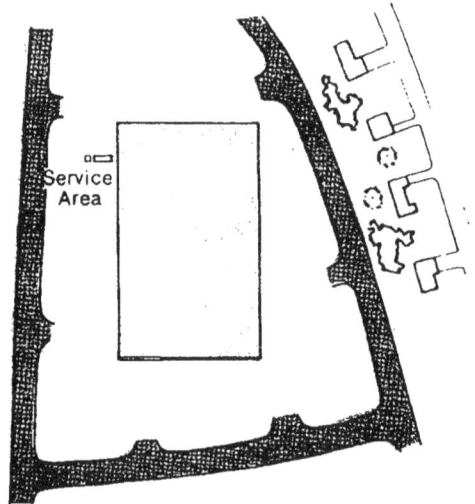

MALL — results in better equalization in store locations, and is good for centralized utility service with service access to stores provided by a truck tunnel under the mall (or service courts).

ARRANGEMENT OF BUILDINGS

- Stores requiring a large number of parking spaces should be placed far apart when possible.

- Shops complementing each other, such as retail stores offering shopping goods, should be located close together for convenience and comparison. Other separate groupings should include convenience outlets and service facilities. Food stores, especially commissaries, should be well separated from comparison shopping outlets.

- Service offices should be located to one side or apart from the main body of the shopping center so that shoppers and persons seeking services mix as little as possible.

- Service stations in community centers are fitting and proper if their locations do not interfere with circulation in the parking lot. Stations should usually be located in a prominent place.

- All community centers should be readily accessible to potential customers. If a large number of customers are contemplated, the center should be located near more than one important roadway.

- Often it is desirable or necessary to build a community center by stages. In this case, the best design for a particular location and size often must be modified to allow stage construction. Increased building area must be served by adequate parking facilities.

PARKING

OFF-STREET PARKING AREAS are essential to all community centers. Parking facilities may be located entirely in front of or entirely at the rear of the buildings, or they may be • both in front of and at the rear of the buildings. In some cases, they are on all sides. The decision as to where to locate parking depends on the relative importance of planned shopping and impulse shopping. It has been estimated that peak-load parking conditions occur only 15 to 20 percent of the open-store time. Thus, a relatively small proportion of parking facilities in front of the stores will accommodate all customers most of the time.

PARKING LAYOUT

- ❖ For shopper convenience, parking should be no more than 300 to 350 feet from a building.
- ❖ Parking rows should be perpendicular to buildings for the safety and convenience of pedestrians; however, perpendicular rows less than 130 feet long are not practical. In this case, use rows parallel to the front of the store.
- ❖ Employee and customer parking should not mix; therefore, separate parking facilities should be provided for employees.
- ❖ Pedestrian crossing points should be kept to a minimum, should be well marked and lighted, and should lead directly to the store groups.
- ❖ Occasionally, covered walkways extending into major parking areas are desirable; such walkways should be lighted for nighttime use and may be landscaped.

PARKING ⟹	1. NUMBER OF STALLS
	2. SIZE OF STALLS
	3. OTHER PARKING NEEDS

1. NUMBER OF STALLS

Generally accepted practice has shown that parking facilities should be designed to accommodate all but the 10 highest shopping hours (usually in the pre-Christmas or pre-Easter seasons). The design to accommodate this period would represent a functionally and economically sound level of parking service.

General guidelines for determining the number of required parking spaces are 5 to 10 car spaces per 1,000 feet of gross building space or 2 to 4 square feet of parking space per square foot of gross building space.

In the first method, the required area does not include driveways. The second method provides 400 square feet per car, allocating between 180 and 200 square feet to the parking space; the remaining area is allocated to access and interior drives, and to landscaped and unusable areas. The selection of either method depends on the proportion of auto to walk-in shoppers and on the ratio of gross building space to retail sales area.

2. SIZE OF STALLS

Dimensions or the various parking and aisle arrangements depend on the parking angle and traffic circulation. However, where room is available, stalls should be 10 feet wide, but never less than 9 feet wide. Double-line stall separators, 1-foot apart, are preferable to single-line stall separators for high-turnover parking as they insure better vehicle positioning in the stall. Aisles that accommodate heavy circulation movements should be 10 feet wider than those normally required.

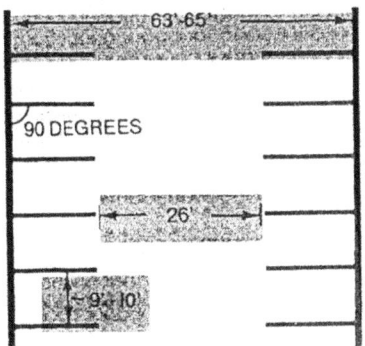

3. OTHER PARKING NEEDS

LOT CIRCULATION

Direction or traffic flow through a community center is a matter of preference and is influenced by the layout of the buildings. Although two-way movement is preferred by the patron, one-way movement is more efficient; however, neither movement appears to be safer than the other. Also, parking directly in front of stores, which is convenient for patrons, influences lot circulation by creating congestion.

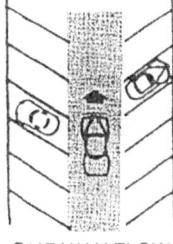 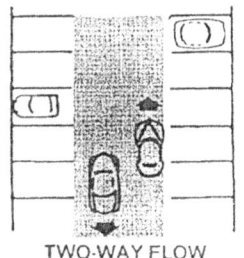

ONE-WAY FLOW   TWO-WAY FLOW

TRUCK SERVICE AREAS

In the layout of truck service areas and truck access roads, every effort should be made to keep them separate from pedestrian areas and customer parking. However, truck service areas, such as in the strip layout, can be made to the rear of the buildings. Service courts can be used efficiently for service with all layouts. In a cluster-type center, truck service easily can be provided in the center of the cluster. However, truck service to a mall design cannot be to the center or to the outside without customer-service conflict and unsightliness. The best, but most costly, truck service for a mall is by tunnel to the building basements. In layouts where truck and patron mixing cannot be avoided, the problem can be minimized by rigid control of time allocation for in and out truck delivery. However, this method is likely to prove inadequate.

LANDSCAPING

Although the essential purpose of the center is to provide shops and services for the patron, landscaping makes a valuable contribution. The objective of landscaping should be to create focal points of beauty, to provide a buffer zone between adjacent land uses, and to subdivide large parking areas.

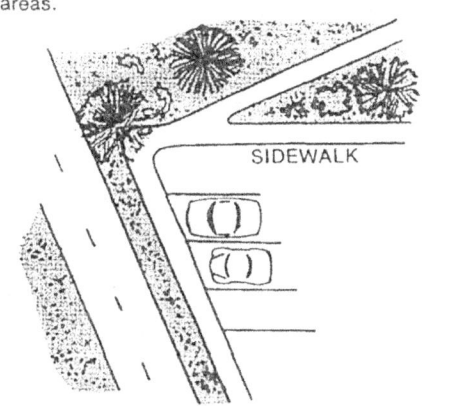

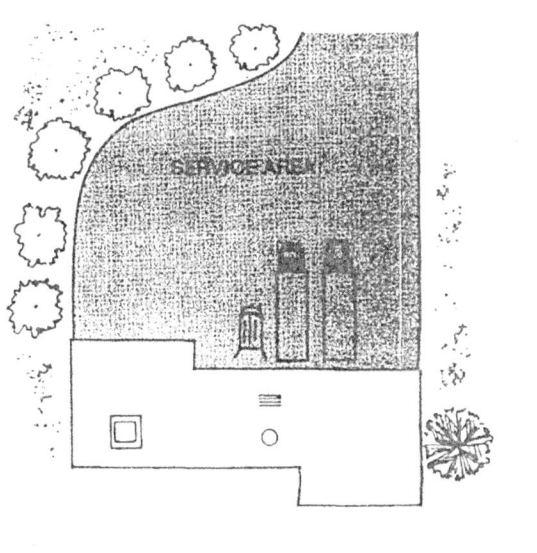

II. WORK SITES

The problem of providing adequate parking facilities for employees is one that should concern both the installation planner and the individual worker. At existing facilities, many signs point to inadequate employee parking. Most give clear evidence of unsafe and inefficient conditions that can be corrected.

Overflow parking occurs in driveways, on-streets, and in other available but unauthorized places. With this unregulated parking, pick-up areas for carpool members or for cars driven by employee family members often are inadequate. Illegal parking in aisles, disregard of directional signs and markings, and vacant parking stalls, indicate inefficient design. Improperly designed sidewalks, crosswalks, loading zones, and parking locations encourage conflicts between pedestrians and vehicles. Long delays at entrances and exits, and long walking distances encourage unsafe driver and pedestrian practices.

PARKING DEMAND
DESIGN PARKING DEMAND TO ACCOMMODATE 70% OF THE EMPLOYMENT

Traffic generation, as discussed in chapter 3, can be used to determine the peak volume of cars to be parked and the peak volume of traffic to be moved onto the installation road network. PARKING DEMAND AT A WORK LOCATION is defined as **the maximum accumulation of vehicles parked** at one time. Because parking demand correlates well with employment, the number of employees may be used to predict demand. The relationship of parking demand to employment is generally around 0.6 spaces per employee. However, for design, a yardstick value of 0.7 spaces per employee is desirable. This higher ratio allows supply to exceed demand, thus reducing the search for the last available space. If it takes too long to find a space, the employee will park illegally.

PARKING ESTIMATES

- **Obtain employment by category: executive, Office, operational.**
- **Estimate parking requirements of each employment category, considering transit usage and car occupancy.**
- **Analyze shift start and end times to determine maximum parking demand.**
- **Allow a contingency of 5 to 10 percent for seasonal fluctuation, inefficient space usage, overtime schedules, and visitor parking.**

THE PEAK-HOUR DEMAND

DESIGN PARKING DEMA ND TO ACCOMMODATE 70% OF THE EMPLOYMENT

THE PEAK-HOUR DEMAND at a work location is essential in estimating the traffic impact on the adjacent street system and in providing efficient ingress and egress. **The peak-hour demand** can be expressed as a proportion of vehicles per maximum shift employee. For design purposes, an estimate of 0.4 to 0.6 vehicles per maximum shift employee arriving in the peak hour can be used to estimate traffic demand. If shifts are not staggered, the higher figure is generally appropriate. On the other hand, the lower hourly rate is more suitable where shifts are staggered.

SITE SELECTION

Among the many factors influencing the choice of a work site that of employee parking and access should not be overlooked. Employee on-street parking reduces street capacity and is a hindrance to traffic flow; therefore, sufficient space should be available to provide off-street parking. When assessing work locations, it should be remembered that employee travel has an important influence on the street system.

Where possible, major facilities should be located on collector streets, and employee traffic should not use local residential streets. Also, the number and location of entrance/exit drives depend on the external roadway system as well as on the internal lot circulation. It may be desirable or even necessary, to distribute peak-hour volumes among several streets to avoid overtaxing the capacity of nearby intersections.

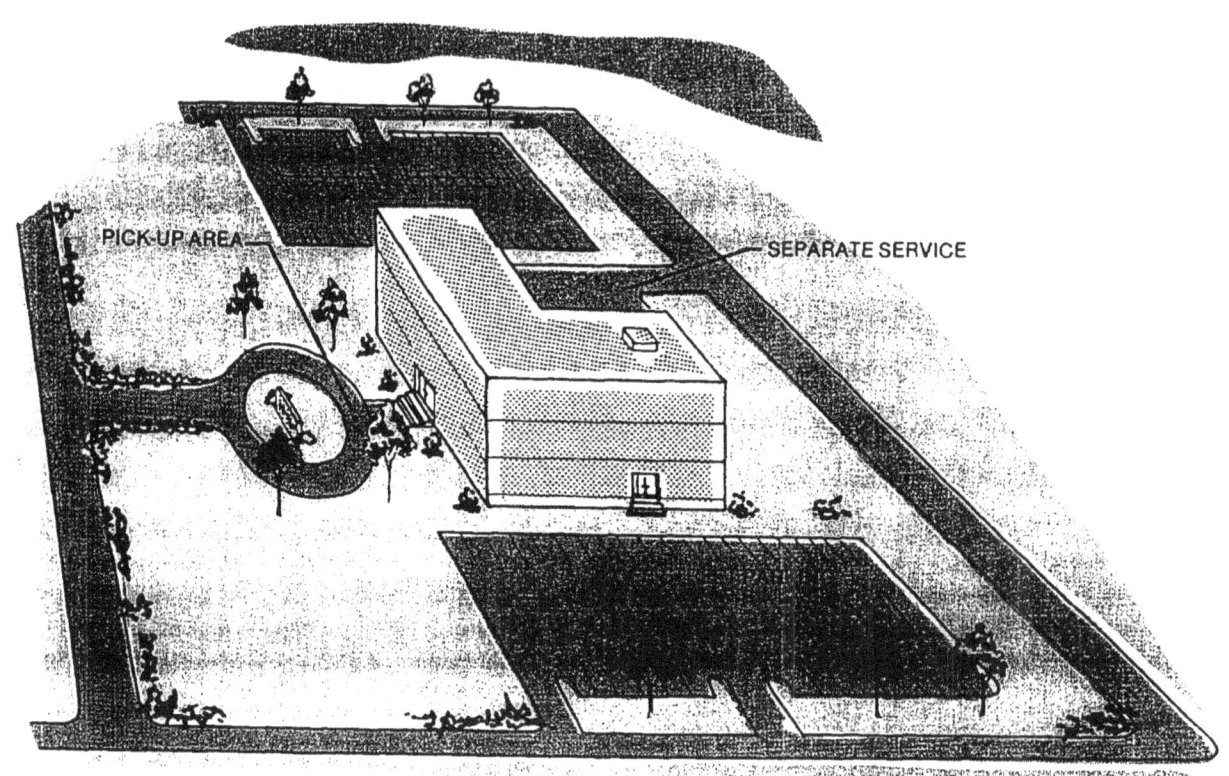

PARKING DESIGN

Unlike parking at community centers, **employee parking is long-term** and is characterized by the nearly simultaneous arrival and departure of many vehicles and by brief periods of vehicle-pedestrian conflict.

Vehicle dimensions are the principal determinant of stall size. Current practice is to employ 9-foot-wide stalls, with 10 foot-wide stalls in some 90-degree visitor parking layouts. If stall widths are less than 9 feet, double lines between stalls should be used to assure better positioning of vehicles.

Stall lengths must be at least 18 feet; however, if drive-through parking is used, stall lengths may be increased to 19 feet to allow for clearance between vehicles. Clearance from walls, fences, roadways, or walkways can be maintained by using curbs or wheel-stops properly positioned within the stall area. A front overhang of 3 feet and a rear overhang of 5 feet are typical.

Decisions on the angle of stall and the layout of aisles must be based on individual site conditions, such as placement and number of entrances and exits, and on site shape and contour. For large parking areas, blocks limiting parking to between 300 and 500 cars are preferable to larger blocks. Pedestrian-vehicle conflicts can be reduced, and assigned parking can be better controlled through use of relatively small blocks.

PEDESTRIAN NEEDS

- Allocate parking space to specific buildings.
- Design parking areas to avoid crossing major roads and to include major walkways.
- Designate major crosswalks by pavement markings, signs, flashing lights, or traffic signals, depending on pedestrian and vehicular volumes. To make them visible to drivers, crosswalk surfaces may be raised slightly unless drainage problems would result.
- Arrange parking aisles to lead directly to buildings. This layout will minimize inbound problems since proximate spaces will be taken first and late arrivals will park farther away. Pedestrians can then walk past parked cars rather than cross aisles when arriving motorists are parking.
- Construct overpasses or underpasses at key crossing points. Grade separation may be essential to prevent long delays and time losses. For example, they may be necessary where parking facilities and office buildings are on opposite sides of a major roadway and also where intersection capacity problems preclude pedestrian phases in traffic signals. However, before such facilities are constructed, careful analysis should be made to determine if they are warranted and if, when constructed, they would be used.

GLOSSARY OF REAL ESTATE TERMS

CONTENTS

	Page
Abstract of Title................Appraisal by Summation	1
Appurtenance........................Cancellation Clause	2
Caveat Emptor................................Conveyance	3
County Clerk's Certificate.... Documentary Evidence	4
Duress......................................Exclusive Agency	5
Exclusive Right to Sell......................Ground Rent	6
Habendum Clause................................ Landlord	7
Lease..Mortgagee	8
Mortgagor..Party Wall	9
Percentage Lease..................................Release	10
Release Clause.....................Subordination Clause	11
Subscribing Witness..............................Valuation	12
Vendee's Lien.... ....Zoning Ordinance	13

GLOSSARY OF REAL ESTATE TERMS

A

Abstract of Title—A summary of all of the recorded instruments and proceedings which affect the title to property, arranged in chronological order.

Accretion—The addition to land through processes of nature, as by streams or wind.

Accrued Interest—Accrue: to grow; to be added to. Accrued interest is interest that has been earned but not due and payable.

Acknowledgment—A formal declaration before a duly authorized officer by a person who has executed an instrument that such execution is the person's act and deed.

Acquisition—An act or process by which a person procures property.

Acre—A measure of land equaling 160 square rods or 4,840 square yards or 43,560 feet.

Adjacent—Lying near to but not necessarily in actual contact with.

Adjoining—Contiguous; attaching, in actual contact with.

Administrator—A person appointed by court to administer the estate of a deceased person who left no will; i.e., who died intestate.

Ad Valorem—According to valuation.

Adverse Possession—A means of acquiring title where an occupant has been in actual, open, notorious, exclusive, and continuous occupancy of property under a claim of right for the required statutory period.

Affidavit—A statement or declaration reduced to writing, and sworn to or affirmed before some officer who is authorized to administer an oath or affirmation.

Affirm—To confirm, to ratify, to verify.

Agency—That relationship between principal and agent which arises out of a contract either expressed or implied, written or oral, wherein an agent is employed by a person to do certain acts on the person's behalf in dealing with a third party.

Agent—One who undertakes to transact some business or to manage some affair for another by authority of the latter.

Agreement of Sale—A written agreement between seller and purchaser in which the purchaser agrees to buy certain real estate and the seller agrees to sell upon terms and conditions set forth therein.

Alienation—A transferring of property to another; the transfer of property and possession of lands, or other things, from one person to another

Amortization—A gradual paying off of a debt by periodical installments.

Apportionments—Adjustment of the income, expenses or carrying charges of real estate usually computed to the date of closing of title so that the seller pays all expenses to that date. The buyer assumes all expenses commencing the date the deed is conveyed to the buyer.

Appraisal—An estimate of a property's valuation by an appraiser who is usually presumed to be expert in this work.

Appraisal by Capitalization—An estimate of value by capitalization of productivity and income.

Appraisal by Comparison—Comparability with the sale prices of other similar properties.

Appraisal by Summation—Adding together all parts of a property separately appraised to form a whole: e.g., value of the land considered as vacant added to the cost of reproduction of the building, less depreciation.

Appurtenance—Something which is outside the property itself but belongs to the land and adds to its greater enjoyment such as a right of way or a barn or a dwelling.

Assessed Valuation—A valuation placed upon property by a public officer or a board, as a basis for taxation.

Assessment—A charge against real estate made by a unit of government to cover a proportionate cost of an improvement such as a street or sewer.

Assessor—An official who has the responsibility of determining assessed values.

Assignee—The person to whom an agreement or contract is assigned.

Assignment—The method or manner by which a right, a specialty, or contract is transferred from one person to another.

Assignor—A party who assigns or transfers an agreement or contract to another.

Assumption of Mortgage—The taking of title to property by a grantee, wherein the grantee assumes liability for payment of an existing note or bond secured by a mortgage against a property and becomes personally liable for the payment of such mortgage debt.

Attest—To witness to; to witness by observation and signature.

Avulsion—The removal of land from one owner to another, when a stream suddenly changes its channel.

B

Beneficiary—The person who receives or is to receive the benefits resulting from certain acts.

Bequeath—To give or hand down by will; to leave by will.

Bequest—That which is given by the terms of a will.

Bill of Sale—A written instrument given to pass title of personal property from vendor to vendee.

Binder—An agreement to cover the down payment for the purchase of real estate as evidence of good faith on the part of the purchaser.

Blanket Mortgage—A single mortgage which covers more than one piece of real estate.

Bona Fide—In good faith, without fraud.

Bond—The evidence of a personal debt which is secured by a mortgage or other lien on real estate.

Building Codes—Regulations established by local governments stating fully the structural requirements for building.

Building Line—A line fixed at a certain distance from the front and/or sides of a lot, beyond which no building can project.

Building Loan Agreement—An agreement whereby the lender advances money to an owner with provisional payments at certain stages of construction.

C

Cancellation Clause—A provision in a lease which confers upon one or more or all of the parties to the lease the right to terminate the party's or parties' obligations thereunder upon the occurrence of the condition or contingency set forth in the said clause.

Caveat Emptor—Let the buyer beware. The buyer must examine the goods or property and buy at the buyer's own risk.

Cease and Desist Order—An order executed by the Secretary of State directing broker recipients to cease and desist from all solicitation of homeowners whose names and addresses appear on the list(s) forwarded with such order. The order acknowledges petition filings by homeowners listed evidencing their premises are not for sale, thereby revoking the implied invitation to solicit. The issuance of a Cease and Desist Order does not prevent an owner from selling or listing his premises for sale. It prohibits soliciting by licensees served with such order and subjects violators to penalties of suspension or revocation of their licenses as provided in section 441-c of the Real Property Law.

Cease and Desist Petition—A statement filed by a homeowner showing address of premises owned which notifies the Department of State that such premises are not for sale and does not wish to be solicited. In so doing, petitioner revokes the implied invitation to be solicited, by any means with respect thereto, by licensed real estate brokers and salespersons.

Certiorari—A proceeding to review in a competent court the action of an inferior tribunal board or officer exercising judicial functions.

Chain of Title—A history of conveyances and encumbrances affecting a title from the time the original patent was granted, or as far back as records are available.

Chattel—Personal property, such as household goods or fixtures.

Chattel Mortgage—A mortgage on personal property.

Client—The one by whom a broker is employed and by whom the broker will be compensated on completion of the purpose of the agency.

Closing Date—The date upon which the buyer takes over the property; usually between 30 and 60 days after the signing of the contract. Cloud on the Title An outstanding claim or encumbrance which, if valid, would affect or impair the owner's title.

Collateral—Additional security pledged for the payment of an obligation.

Color of Title—That which appears to be good title, but which is not title in fact.

Commission—A sum due a real estate broker for services in that capacity.

Commitment—A pledge or a promise or affirmation agreement.

Condemnation—Taking private property for public use, with fair compensation to the owner; exercising the right of eminent domain.

Conditional Sales Contract—A contract for the sale of property stating that delivery is to be made to the buyer, title to remain vested in the seller until the conditions of the contract have been fulfilled.

Consideration—Anything of value given to induce entering into a contract; it may be money, personal services, or even love and affection.

Constructive Notice—Information or knowledge of a fact imputed by law to a person because the person could have discovered the fact by proper diligence and inquiry; (public records).

Contract—An agreement between competent parties to do or not to do certain things for a legal consideration, whereby each party acquires a right to what the other possesses.

Conversion—Change from one character or use to another.

Conveyance—The transfer of the title of land from one to another. The means or medium by which title of real estate is transferred.

County Clerk's Certificate—When an acknowledgment is taken by an officer not authorized in the state or county where the document is to be recorded, the instrument which must be attached to the acknowledgment is called a county clerk's certificate. It is given by the clerk of the county where the officer obtained his/her authority and certifies to the officer's signature and powers.

Covenants—Agreements written into deeds and other instruments promising performance or nonperformance of certain acts, or stipulating certain uses or nonuse's of the property.

D

Damages—The indemnity recoverable by a person who has sustained an injury, either to his/her person, property or relative rights, through the act or default of another.

Decedent—One who is dead.

Decree Order issued by one in authority; an edict or law; a judicial decision.

Dedication—A grant and appropriation of land by its owner for some public use, accepted for such use, by an authorized public official on behalf of the public.

Deed—An instrument in writing duly executed and delivered, that conveys title to real property.

Deed Restriction—An imposed restriction in a deed for the purpose of limiting the use of the land such as: A restriction against the sale of liquor thereon. A restriction As to the size, type, value or placement of improvements that may be erected thereon.

Default—Failure to fulfill a duty or promise, or to discharge an obligation; omission or failure to perform any acts.

Defendant—The party sued or called to answer in any suit, civil or criminal, at law or in equity.

Deficiency Judgment—A judgment given when the security for a loan does not entirely satisfy the debt upon its default.

Delivery—The transfer of the possession of a thing from one person to another.

Demising Clause—A clause found in a lease whereby the landlord (lessor) leases and the tenant (lessee) takes the property.

Depreciation—Loss of value in real property brought about by age, physical deterioration, or functional or economic obsolescence.

Descent—When an owner of real estate dies intestate, the owner's property descends, by operation of law, to the owner's distributees.

Devise—A gift of real estate by will or last testament.

Devisee—One who receives a bequest of real estate made by will.

Devisor—One who bequeaths real estate by will.

Directional Growth—The location or direction toward which the residential sections of a city are destined or determined to grow.

Dispossess Proceedings—Summary process by a landlord to oust a tenant and regain possession of the premises for nonpayment of rent or other breach of conditions of the lease or occupancy.

Distributee—Person receiving or entitled to receive land as representative of the former owner.

Documentary Evidence—Evidence in the form of written or printed papers.

Duress—Unlawful constraint exercised upon a person whereby the person is forced to do some act against his will.

Earnest Money—Down payment made by a purchaser of real estate as evidence of good faith.

Easement—A right that may be exercised by the public or individuals on, over or through the lands of others.

Ejectment—A form of action to regain possession of real property, with damages for the unlawful retention; used when there is no relationship of landlord and tenant.

Eminent Domain—A right of the government to acquire property for necessary public use by condemnation; the owner must be fairly compensated.

Encroachment—A building, part of a building, or obstruction which intrudes upon or invades a highway or sidewalk or trespasses upon the property of another.

Encumbrance—Any right to or interest in land that diminishes its value. (Also Incumbrance)

Endorsement—An act of signing one's name on the back of a check or note, with or without further qualifications.

Equity—The interest or value which the owner has in real estate over and above the liens against it.

Equity of Redemption—A right of the owner to reclaim property before it is sold through foreclosure proceedings, by the payment of the debt, interest and costs.

Erosion—The wearing away of land through processes of nature, as by streams and winds.

Escheat—The reversion to the state of property in event the owner thereof dies, without leaving a will and has no distributees to whom the property may pass by lawful descent.

Escrow—A written agreement between two or more parties providing that certain instruments or property be placed with a third party to be delivered to a designated person upon the fulfillment or performance of some act or condition.

Estate—The degree, quantity, nature and extent of interest which a person has in real property.

Estate for Life—An estate or interest held during the terms of some certain person's life.

Estate in Reversion—The residue of an estate left for the grantor, to commence in possession after the termination of some particular estate granted by the grantor.

Estate at Will—The occupation of lands and tenements by a tenant for an indefinite period, terminable by one or both parties at will.

Estoppel Certificate—An instrument executed by the mortgagor setting forth the present status and the balance due on the mortgage as of the date of the execution of the certificate. A legal proceeding by a lessor landlord to recover possession of real property.

Eviction, Actual—Where one is, either by force or by process of law, actually put out of possession.

Eviction, Constructive—Any disturbance of the tenant's possessions by the landlord whereby the premises are rendered unfit or unsuitable for the purpose for which they were leased.

Eviction, Partial—Where the possessor of the premises is deprived of a portion thereof.

Exclusive Agency—An agreement of employment of a broker to the exclusion of all other brokers; if sale is made by any other broker during term of employment, broker holding exclusive agency is entitled to commissions in addition to the commissions payable to the broker who effected the transaction.

Exclusive Right to Sell—An agreement of employment by a broker under which the exclusive right to sell for a specified period is granted to the broker; if a sale during the term of the agreement is made by the owner or by any other broker, the broker holding such exclusive right to sell is nevertheless entitled to compensation.

Executor—A male person or a corporate entity or any other type of organization named or designated in a will to carry out its provisions as to the disposition of the estate of a deceased person.

Executrix—A woman appointed to perform the duties similar to those of an executor.

Extension Agreement—An agreement which extends the life of the mortgage to a later date.

F

Fee; Fee Simple; Fee Absolute—Absolute ownership of real property; a person has this type of estate where the person is entitled to the entire property with unconditional power of disposition during the person's life and descending to the person's distributees and legal representatives upon the person's death intestate.

Fiduciary—A person who on behalf of or for the benefit of another transacts business or handles money on property not the person's own; such relationship implies great confidence and trust.

Fixtures—Personal property so attached to the land or improvements as to become part of the real property.

Foreclosure—A procedure whereby property pledged as security for a debt is sold to pay the debt in the event of default in payments or terms.

Forfeiture—Loss of money or anything of value, by way of penalty due to failure to perform.

Freehold—An interest in real estate, not less than an estate for life. (Use of this term discontinued Sept. 1, 1967.)

Front Foot—A standard measurement, one foot wide, of the width of land, applied at the frontage on its street line. Each front foot extends the depth of the lot.

G

Grace Period—Additional time allowed to perform an act or make a payment before a default occurs.

Graduated Leases—A lease which provides for a graduated change at stated intervals in the amount of the rent to be paid; used largely in long term leases.

Grant—A technical term used in deeds of conveyance of lands to indicate a transfer. Grantee The party to whom the title to real property is conveyed.

Grantor—The person who conveys real estate by deed; the seller.

Gross Income—Total income from property before any expenses are deducted.

Gross Lease—A lease of property whereby the lessor is to meet all property charges regularly incurred through ownership.

Ground Rent—Earnings of improved property credited to earning of the ground itself after allowance made for earnings of improvements.

H

Habendum Clause—The "To Have and To Hold" clause which defines or limits the quantity of the estate granted in the premises of the deed.

Hereditaments—The largest classification of property; including lands, tenements and incorporeal property, such as rights of way.

Holdover Tenant—A tenant who remains in possession of leased property after the expiration of the lease term.

Hypothecate—To give a thing as security without the necessity of giving up possession of it.

I

In Rem—A proceeding against the realty directly; as distinguished from a proceeding against a person. (Used in taking land for nonpayment of taxes, etc.)

Incompetent—A person who is unable to manage his/her own affairs by reason of insanity, inbecility or feeble-mindedness.

Incumbrance—Any right to or interest in land that diminishes its value. (Also Encumbrance)

Injunction—A writ or order issued under the seal of a court to restrain one or more parties to a suit or proceeding from doing an act which is deemed to be inequitable or unjust in regard to the rights of some other party or parties in the suit or proceeding.

Installments—Parts of the same debt, payable at successive periods as agreed; payments made to reduce a mortgage.

Instrument—A written legal document; created to effect the rights of the parties. Interest

Rate—The percentage of a sum of money charged for its use.

Intestate—A person who dies having made no will, or leaves one which is defective in form, in which case the person's estate descends to the person's distributees.

Involuntary Lien—A lien imposed against property without consent of the owner, i.e., taxes, special assessments.

Irrevocable—Incapable of being recalled or revoked; unchangeable; unalterable.

J

Jeopardy—Peril, danger.

Joint Tenancy—Ownership of realty by two or more persons, each of whom has an undivided interest with the "right of survivorship."

Judgment—Decree of a court declaring that one individual is indebted to another, and fixing the amount of such indebtedness.

Junior Mortgage—A mortgage second in lien to a previous mortgage.

L

Laches—Delay or negligence in asserting one's legal rights.

Land, Tenements and Hereditaments—A phrase used in the early English Law, to express all sorts of property of the immovable class.

Landlord—One who rents property to another.

Lease—A contract whereby, for a consideration, usually termed rent, one who is entitled to the possession of real property transfers such rights to another for life, for a term of years, or at will. Leasehold The interest or estate which a lessee of real estate has therein by virtue of the lessee's lease.

Lessee—A person to whom property is rented under a lease.

Lessor—One who rents property to another under a lease.

Lien—A legal right or claim upon a specific property which attaches to the property until a debt is satisfied.

Lien (Mechanic's)—A notice filed with the County Clerk stating that payment has not been made for an improvement to real property. Life Estate The conveyance of title to property for the duration of the life of the grantee.

Life Tenant—The holder of a life estate.

Lis Pendens—A legal document, filed in the office of the county clerk giving notice that an action or proceeding is pending in the courts affecting the title to the property.

Listing—An employment contract between principal and agent, authorizing the agent to perform services for the principal involving the latter's property.

Litigation—The act of carrying on a lawsuit.

M

Mandatory—Requiring strict conformity or obedience.

Market Value—The highest price which a buyer, willing but not compelled to buy, would pay, and the lowest a seller, willing but not compelled to sell, would accept.

Marketable Title—A title which a court of equity considers to be so free from defect that it will enforce its acceptance by a purchaser.

Mechanic's Lien—A lien given by law upon a building or other improvement upon land, and upon the land itself, to secure the price of labor done upon, and materials furnished for, the improvement.

Meeting of the Minds—Whenever all parties to a contract agree to the exact terms thereof.

Metes and Bounds—A term used in describing the boundary lines of land, setting forth all the boundary lines together with their terminal points and angles.

Minor—A person under an age specified by law; under 18 years of age.

Monument—A fixed object and point established by surveyors to establish land locations.

Moratorium—An emergency act by a legislative body to suspend the legal enforcement of contractual obligations.

Mortgage—An instrument in writing, duly executed and delivered, that creates a lien upon real estate as security for the payment of a specified debt, which is usually in the form of a bond.

Mortgage Commitment—A formal indication, by a lending institution that it will grant a mortgage loan on property, in a certain specified amount and on certain specified terms. Mortgage Reduction Certificate An instrument executed by the mortgagee, setting forth the present status and the balance due on the mortgage as of the date of the execution of the instrument.

Mortgagee—The party who lends money and takes a mortgage to secure the payment thereof.

Mortgagor—A person who borrows money and gives a mortgage on the person's property as security for the payment of the debt.

Multiple Listing—An arrangement among Real Estate Board of Exchange Members, whereby each broker presents the broker's listings to the attention of the other members so that if a sale results, the commission is divided between the broker bringing the listing and the broker making the sale.

N

Net Listing—A price below which an owner will not sell the property, and at which price a broker will not receive a commission; the broker receives the excess over and above the net listing as the broker's commission.

Notary Public—A public officer who is authorized to take acknowledgments to certain classes of documents, such as deeds, contracts, mortgages, and before whom affidavits may be sworn.

O

Obligee—The person in whose favor an obligation is entered into.

Obligor—The person who binds himself/herself to another; one who has engaged to perform some obligation; one who makes a bond.

Obsolescence—Loss in value due to reduced desirability and usefulness of a structure because its design and construction become obsolete; loss because of becoming old-fashioned, and not in keeping with modern means, with consequent loss of income.

Open End Mortgage—A mortgage under which the mortgagor may secure additional funds from the mortgagee, usually up to but not exceeding the original amount of the existing amortizing mortgage.

Open Listing—A listing given to any number of brokers without liability to compensate any except the one who first secures a buyer ready, willing and able to meet the terms of the listing, or secures the acceptance by the seller of a satisfactory offer; the sale of the property automatically terminates the listing.

Open Mortgage—A mortgage that has matured or is overdue and, therefore, is "open" to foreclosure at any time.

Option—A right given for a consideration to purchase or lease a property upon specified terms within a specified time; if the right is not exercised the option holder is not subject to liability for damages; if exercised, the grantor of option must perform.

P

Partition—The division which is made of real property between those who own it in undivided shares.

Party Wall—A party wall is a wall built along the line separating two properties, partly on each, which wall either owner, the owner's heirs and assigns has the right to use; such right constituting an easement over so much of the adjoining owner's land as is covered by the wall.

Percentage Lease—A lease of property in which the rental is based upon the percentage of the volume of sales made upon the leased premises, usually provides for minimum rental.
Personal Property—Any property which is not real property.
Plat Book—A public record containing maps of land showing the division of such land into streets, blocks and lots and indicating the measurements of the individual parcels.
Plottage—Increment in unity value of a plot of land created by assembling smaller ownerships into one ownership.
Police Power—The right of any political body to enact laws and enforce them, for the order, safety, health, morals and general welfare of the public.
Power of Attorney—A written instrument duly signed and executed by an owner of property, which authorizes an agent to act on behalf of the owner to the extent indicated in the instrument.
Premises—Lands and tenements; an estate; the subject matter of a conveyance.
Prepayment Clause—A clause in a mortgage which gives a mortgagor the privilege of paying the mortgage indebtedness before it becomes due.
Principal—The employer of an agent or broker; the broker's or agent's client.
Probate—To establish the will of a deceased person.
Purchase Money Mortgage—A mortgage given by a grantee in part payment of the purchase price of real estate.

Q

Quiet Enjoyment—The right of an owner or a person legally in possession to the use of property without interference of possession.
Quiet Title Suit—A suit in court to remove a defect, cloud or suspicion regarding legal rights of an owner to a certain parcel of real property.
Quitclaim Deed—A deed which conveys simply the grantor's rights or interest in real estate, without any agreement or covenant as to the nature or extent of that interest, or any other covenants; usually used to remove a cloud from the title.

R

Real Estate Board—An organization whose members consist primarily of real estate brokers and salespersons.
Real Property—Land, and generally whatever is erected upon or affixed thereto.
Realtor—A coined word which may only be used by an active member of a local real estate board, affiliated with the National Association of Real Estate Boards.
Recording—The act of writing or entering in a book of public record instruments affecting the title to real property.
Redemption—The right of a mortgagor to redeem the property by paying a debt after the expiration date and before sale at foreclosure; the right of an owner to reclaim the owner's property after the sale for taxes.
Release—The act or writing by which some claim or interest is surrendered to another.

Release Clause—A clause found in a blanket mortgage which gives the owner of the property the privilege of paying off a portion of the mortgage indebtedness, and thus freeing a portion of the property from the mortgage.

Rem—(See In Rem)

Remainder—An estate which takes effect after the termination of a prior estate such as a life estate.

Remainderman—The person who is to receive the property after the death of a life tenant.

Rent—The compensation paid for the use of real estate.

Reproduction Cost—Normal cost of exact duplication of a property as of a certain date.

Restriction—A limitation placed upon the use of property contained in the deed or other written instrument in the chain of title. Reversionary Interest The interest which a person has in lands or other property upon the termination of the preceding estate.

Revocation—An act of recalling a power of authority conferred, as the revocation of a power of attorney, a license, an agency, etc.

Right of Survivorship—Right of the surviving joint owner to succeed to the interests of the deceased joint owner, distinguishing feature of a joint tenancy or tenancy by the entirety.

Right of Way—The right to pass over another's land more or less frequently according to the nature of the easement.

Riparian Owner—One who owns land bounding upon a river or watercourse.

Riparian Rights—The right of a landowner to water on, under or adjacent to his land.

S

Sales Contract—A contract by which the buyer and seller agree to terms of sale.

Satisfaction Piece—An instrument for recording and acknowledging payment of an indebtedness secured by a mortgage.

Seizin—The possession of land by one who claims to own at least an estate for life therein.

Set Back—The distance from the curb or other established line, within which no buildings may be erected.

Severalty—The ownership of real property by an individual, as an individual.

Special Assessment—An assessment made against a property to pay for a public improvement by which the assessed property is supposed to be especially benefited.

Specific Performance—A remedy in a court of equity compelling a defendant to carry out the terms of an agreement or contract.

Statute—A law established by an act of the Legislature.

Statute of Frauds—State law which provides that certain contracts must be in writing in order to be enforceable at law.

Stipulations—The terms within a written contract.

Straight Line Depreciation—A definite sum set aside annually from income to pay costs of replacing improvements, without reference to the interest it earns.

Subdivision—A tract of land divided into lots or plots suitable for home building purposes.

Subletting—A leasing by a tenant to another, who holds under the tenant.

Subordination Clause—A clause which permits the placing of a mortgage at a later date which takes priority over an existing mortgage.

Subscribing Witness—One who writes his/her name as witness to the execution of an instrument.

Surety—One who guarantees the performance of another; guarantor.

Surrender—The cancellation of a lease by mutual consent of the lessor and the lessee.

Surrogate's Court (Probate Court)—A court having jurisdiction over the proof of wills, the settling of estates and of citations.

Survey—The process by which a parcel of land is measured and its area ascertained; also the blueprint showing the measurements, boundaries and area.

T

Tax Sale—Sale of property after a period of nonpayment of taxes.

Tenancy in Common—An ownership of realty by two or more persons, each of whom has an undivided interest, without the "right of survivorship."

Tenancy by the Entirety—An estate which exists only between husband and wife with equal right of possession and enjoyment during their joint lives and with the "right of survivorship."

Tenancy at Will—A license to use or occupy lands and tenements at the will of the owner.

Tenant—One who is given possession of real estate for a fixed period or at will.

Tenant at Sufferance—One who comes into possession of lands by lawful title and keeps it afterwards without any title at all.

Testate—Where a person dies leaving a valid will.

Title—Evidence that owner of land is in lawful possession thereof; evidence of ownership.

Title Insurance—A policy of insurance which indemnifies the holder for any loss sustained by reason of defects in the title.

Title Search—An examination of the public records to determine the ownership and encumbrances affecting real property.

Torrens Title—System of title records provided by state law: it is a system for the registration of land titles whereby the state of the title, showing ownership and encumbrances, can be readily ascertained from an inspection of the "register of titles" without the necessity of a search of the public records.

Tort—A wrongful act, wrong, injury; violation of a legal right.

Transfer Tax—A tax charged under certain conditions on the property belonging to an estate.

U

Unearned Increment—An increase in value of real estate due to no effort on the part of the owner; often due to increase in population.

Urban Property—City property; closely settled property.

Usury—On a loan, claiming a rate of interest greater than that permitted by law.

V

Valid—Having force, or binding force; legally sufficient and authorized by law.

Valuation—Estimated worth or price. The act of valuing by appraisal.

Vendee's Lien—A lien against property under contract of sale to secure deposit paid by a purchaser.

Verification—Sworn statements before a duly qualified officer to the correctness of the contents of an instrument.

Violations—Act, deed or conditions contrary to law or permissible use of real property.

Void—To have no force or effect; that which is unenforceable.

Voidable—That which is capable of being adjudged void, but is not void unless action is taken to make it so.

W

Waiver—The renunciation, abandonment or surrender of some claim, right or privilege.

Warranty Deed—A conveyance of land in which the grantor warrants the title to the grantee.

Will—The disposition of one's property to take effect after death.

Without Recourse—Words used in endorsing a note or bill to denote that the future holder is not to look to the endorser in case of nonpayment.

Z

Zone—An area set off by the proper authorities for specific use; subject to certain restrictions or restraints.

Zoning Ordinance—Act of city or county or other authorities specifying type and use to which property may be put in specific areas.

www.ingramcontent.com/pod-product-compliance
Lightning Source LLC
Chambersburg PA
CBHW081820300426
44116CB00014B/2427